This book will help many people and organisations ... in a simple way, it makes the reader understand the risks of bad project management decisions and gives a complete ... understanding of the strengths, weaknesses, opportunities, and threats in projects.

– Sergio P. Capitine, Mechanical Engineer,
Project Manager at BP Mozambique

The concept of Operational Readiness lies at the heart of systems development. Awareness of it should be maintained throughout the SDLC ... A book that is easy to read and a "must-have" for system developers from all walks of life.

– Tapiwa Bande (MEng),
Managing Director of African Hard Systems (Pty) Ltd

A comprehensive treatise on Operational Readiness ... OR and PIR Planning are indeed business activities ... operability failure may lead to business failure.

– Saseka Vara, Chartered Accountant,
Senior Manager at Transnet SOC

Operational Readiness

This book offers a guide on how to prepare business and operational environments to safely receive and effectively utilise systems (i.e., products of projects) to prevent successfully completed systems from failing to add value to their intended environment. It is supplemented with four extended practical exercises to help readers apply the principles to their own large, complex projects and ensure project success.

Operational Readiness remains one of the least developed practices of both Project Management (PM) and Systems Engineering (SE). As a result, satisfactorily completed "systems" (e.g., satellites, aircrafts, mine shafts, power plants, road and rail networks, hospitals, and schools), completed on time, on budget, and to specification, are often failing to add value by providing improvements in their intended operational environment. In numerous cases, System Deployment is also accompanied by adverse and detrimental effects on the business and operational environments, and at times on the broader environment (e.g., persistent pollution, negative economic externalities, exacerbation of social ills such as deprivation and crime). In this book, the author discusses both the process and challenges of deploying the product into its intended operational environment and offers guidance to enable organisations to benefit from a holistic framework for Operational Readiness.

This forward-thinking book is essential reading for all those involved with managing large projects including project managers, sponsors, and executives. It will also be useful for advanced students of Project Management and Systems Engineering looking to understand and expand their knowledge of Operational Readiness, infrastructure projects, and systems deployment.

Pascal Bohulu Mabelo has more than 20 years of professional experience and possesses a wide range of technical and managerial skills pertaining to projects. He has previously served as the national chairman of Project Management South Africa (PMSA) and is a regular speaker at Project Management conferences and seminars. He promotes the application of Systems Engineering concepts to unravel complexity in Large Infrastructure Projects.

Operational Readiness

How to Achieve Successful System
Deployment

Pascal Bohulu Mabelo

Routledge
Taylor & Francis Group

LONDON AND NEW YORK

First published 2020 by Routledge

2 Park Square, Milton Park, Abingdon, Oxon OX14 4RN

605 Third Avenue, New York, NY 10017

Routledge is an imprint of the Taylor & Francis Group, an informa business

First issued in paperback 2022

Publisher's Note

The publisher has gone to great lengths to ensure the quality of this
reprint but points out that some imperfections in the original copies
may be apparent.

British Library Cataloguing-in-Publication Data
A catalogue record for this book is available from the British Library

Library of Congress Cataloging-in-Publication Data
Names: Bohulu Mabelo, Pascal, 1969- author.
Title: Operational readiness: how to achieve successful system deployment
/Pascal Bohulu Mabelo.
Description: 1 Edition. | New York: Routledge, 2020. |
Includes bibliographical references and index.
Identifiers: LCCN 2019056619 (print) | LCCN 2019056620 (ebook) |
ISBN 9780367903343 (hardback) | ISBN 9781003023821 (ebook)
Subjects: LCSH: Project management. | Systems engineering. |
Strategic planning | Industrial management.
Classification: LCC HD69.P75 .B634 2020 (print) | LCC HD69.P75 (ebook) |
DDC 658.4/04-dc23
LC record available at https://lccn.loc.gov/2019056619
LC ebook record available at https://lccn.loc.gov/2019056620

ISBN: 978-0-367-90334-3 (hbk)
ISBN: 978-1-03-233648-0 (pbk)
DOI: 10.4324/9781003023821

Typeset in Bembo
by Deanta Global Publishing Services, Chennai, India

To my God-given wife and children,

To the Project Management fraternity across Africa and the Diaspora,

I humbly dedicate this work.

Contents

Figures

Tables

About the author

**Pascal Bohulu Mabelo** MBA, MSc (Eng), Pr Eng (South Africa), Pr CPM (South Africa), PMP

Pascal possesses a wide range of technical and managerial skills pertaining to infrastructure projects and has had the opportunity to work on an array of large-scale projects with people from various backgrounds. He presently works as a principal consultant through his own practice, E 6 Project Consulting (Pty) Ltd, and contracts on diverse assignments in both the private and public sector.

Pascal has worked in large projects as a design engineer, project/programme manager, project consultant, and Project Management executive; he had previously established and for eight years headed up the Project Management Centre of Excellence at the "capital projects" division of a multi-billion company in South Africa. With more than 20 years of professional experience in the industry, he has steadily built up an extensive network in the industry and was honoured to serve as the national chairman of PM South Africa (PMSA), the leading Project Management professional association in Southern Africa.

Pascal is also well known in the industry for having authored several articles in Project Management magazines and journals, and has guest-lectured on project-related processes at various top-ranked South African universities, not to mention speaking at Project Management conferences and seminars. He is currently promoting the application of Systems Thinking and/or Systems Engineering principles and concepts to unravel complexity in Large Infrastructure Projects (LIPs) in order to address their persistent risks of failure – and their massive, pernicious cost and schedule overruns.

About this book

Operational Readiness (OR) falls within the ambit of Systems Engineering (SE) Transition Process and it seeks to assure successful System Deployment of newly built systems. However, even at this juncture, at the dawn of the "Fourth Industrial Revolution", OR remains one of the least developed practices of both Project Management and Systems Engineering.

As a result, satisfactorily completed "systems" (e.g., satellites, aircrafts, mine shafts, power plants, road and rail networks, hospitals, and schools completed on time, on budget, and to specification) are often failing to add value by providing improvements in their intended operational environment. In numerous cases, System Deployment is also accompanied by adverse and detrimental effects on the business and operational environments, and at times on the broader environment (e.g., persistent pollution, negative economic externalities, exacerbation of social ills such as deprivation and crime).

Completing any "system" on time, on budget, and to specification, real-life experience and recent studies suggest, is but a "basis" for improving operations. Notwithstanding the need for any "system" that is being developed to eventually attain maturity (i.e., fully implemented product) and readiness (i.e., fitness for *intended* purpose), the imperative of securing a sustainable "Capability Readiness" is rather achieved by way of eliciting operational requirements from both "system" owners and users at the project outset and, subsequently, by validating that such have been satisfied before the start of operations.

Systems would fail when operations are not "made ready" to safely receive and, thus, efficiently and effectively utilise them. This difficulty largely arises from two situations: (1) the misplaced focus of many lifecycle methodologies on constructability rather than on operability, leading project managers into thinking that their onus ends at Close-Out, and

(2) the absence of a holistic framework for Operational Readiness (OR). This book seeks to address the latter; hence, it discusses the processes and challenges of deploying the Solution-System (product) into its intended operational environment.

In its format and content, this material is devised to meet the needs of various readers:

(i)   Project professionals (to provide them with both knowledge and tools about OR);
(ii) Company executives (to increase awareness of the necessity and benefits of OR);
(iii) Academia (to kindle the desire to undertake further research on the topic of OR).

It is therefore hoped that the above entities will work together to further establish OR.

Foreword

For decades, the "triple constraints" principle (i.e., completing projects on time, on budget, and within specification) has been the bedrock for defining project success. Even though the principle is well known, it is clear that many projects do not deliver value after they have been completed. As the author has pointed out on numerous occasions within this book, the "missing link" at times is the lack of understanding with regard to Operational Readiness: making the organisation ready to safely receive and effectively utilise the "products of projects" (which are systems).

During project execution, project practitioners can be so caught up in the delivery of tasks as per the schedule that they often fail to ask themselves critical questions on Operational Readiness. Hence, the project at times becomes a "white elephant". Moreover, some practitioners may even overlook the implications of Human Capital Readiness as it relates to the project. That is why so many products and services end up not being accepted (by stakeholders) or supported after handover.

It is common knowledge that without people organisations cannot build successful projects or systems. Human Capital Readiness, as pointed out by the author, should become a necessity for the sustainability of the organisation. Having said that, dealing with the "behavioural" component of Operational Readiness is more of an art than science. This might prove a challenge for those practitioners who tend to have a steadfast approach on the "science of projects"; this book will actually assist them as it creates a balance between these rather complementary perspectives.

As the author asserts, Operational Readiness is not an aspect to be considered just before handover, but it should be built in within the project, right through to the end, and verified at Post-Implementation Reviews (PIRs). Like any other profession, Project Management is constantly evolving, and practitioners such as the author are bringing forth the knowledge that is so critical to the effective and efficient running of projects. It is therefore crucial that project practitioners take note and apply the principles articulated in this book – I see its application stretching beyond Project Management!

Dr Lunga Msengana[1]

1   Dr Lunga Msengana is a published author, a Project Portfolio Manager at Eskom Holdings SOC Ltd, and a part-time lecturer at Unisa Graduate School of Business Leadership, South Africa, and at Cranefield College, South Africa.

Acronyms

BIM	Building Information Modelling
EPC/M	Engineering Procurement and Construction/ Management
ERP	Enterprise Resources Planning
ISO	International Organization for Standardization
NASA	National Aeronautics and Space Administration (USA)
NETLIPSE	Network for the Dissemination of Knowledge on the Management and Organisation of Large Infrastructure Projects in Europe
NPV	Net Present Value
PMIS	Project Management Information System
ROCE	Return on Capital Employed
ROI	Return on Investment

1 Introduction

The effective execution of organisational strategies carries the business from a current "alpha" status to a more desirable, more competitive "beta" status. Thus, it brings to organisations the challenges of translating such strategies into project-like initiatives and of relying on proper and effective Project Management to successfully deliver such projects – and poor implementation has been the nemesis of many brilliant strategies.

A global mining company operating in South Africa noted in their 2013 Annual Report: "The Company captures value across the value chain through its commercial and logistics strategies and by executing its growth projects efficiently, while continuing to deliver on its organisational responsibilities, capabilities and societal obligations".

Companies must be aware that until their "growth projects" are satisfactorily delivered, both operations and value creation (i.e., their long-term viability) will be compromised.

At a governmental level, it is estimated that the world will need more infrastructure than any nation can deliver. Long-term projections call for an estimated US$ 57 trillion globally to build new and refurbish existing infrastructure between 2013 and 2030.[58] It is hoped that such infrastructure investments will create jobs and, when completed, those projects will help society increase its wealth and its citizens' standard of living.

Unfortunately, chronic project failures will affect companies and governments in terms of both strategy realisation and financial performance (e.g., adverse impacts on their income statements and balance sheets), as well as the "overall competitiveness" of either entities – poor project performance erodes long-term sustainability. The Independent Project Analysts (IPA) gives a stern warning to companies delivering Large Infrastructure Projects (LIPs), "As we look back over the past 23 years at IPA customers that have disappeared, all but one of them grossly overspent for their capital assets [i.e., LIPs]".[41] It is therefore crucial that projects, large ones in particular, are effectively completed.

Completing any system on time, on budget, and to specifications is necessary but not *sufficient* to assure sustained improvements in the intended operational environment. A successfully completed system that fails to add value to its operational environment is basically a "white elephant", only good for the beholding – it is a "successful failure", with operational expectations not met, and business promises not being delivered.[8]

Newly developed systems should not be deemed successful unless and until they are successfully deployed in their intended operational environment (having transitioned from the project realm to operations, where acquired "capabilities" are exploited) to derive the benefits for the owner-organisation. This looks further than commissioning.

Therefore, "The successful transition of systems to operations and support, which includes maintenance and improvements, depends on clear transition criteria that the stakeholders agreed on", according to the *NASA Handbook of Systems Engineering* (2007).[53] Moreover,

> the purpose of the Transition Process is to establish a capability to provide services specified by stakeholder requirements in the operational environment. This process installs [or else deploys] a verified system, together with relevant enabling systems, e.g., operating system, support system, operator training system, user training system, as defined in agreements.[26]

This applies to all projects, be they power plants, mines, road or railway networks, hospitals, factories, or aircraft.

The transition from the project environment (i.e., where the system is delivered) to the operational environment (i.e., where its capabilities are exploited through ongoing processes focused on sustaining the organisation[27]) generally brings the challenges of "readiness" of the operational functions. Such functions include to manage, operate, maintain, support, and dispose of the deployed system; indeed, "Organizational units cooperate to ... deploy, operate, maintain and dispose of the system-of-interest".[23]

Readiness as a concept originated from the military. It is defined as "The capability of a unit or formation, ship, weapon system, or equipment to perform the missions or functions for which it is organized or designed".[13] It applies to all "systems".[23,51]

The term readiness is used in a general sense or to express a level or degree of readiness to transition to operations; hence, its recent application in capital projects.

Operational Readiness (OR) as a Project Management tool is used to prepare the "operational environment" of the owner-organisation to effectively accommodate the product or solution, and accept changes resulting from a particular (set of) project(s). This OR could prove a decisive factor for project success because, as Al-Ahmad argues, "Few organizations are armed with the necessary infrastructure, education, training, or management discipline to bring project initiatives to successful completion".[2]

(Chapter 9 refers to such organisational items as part of "organisational energy".[6])

The Large Infrastructure Projects industry is strewn with "corpses" of projects that failed due to an inadequate or lack of Operational Readiness. For example, the colossal 2,350-store New South China Mall (Dongguan) was "abandoned" soon after its 2005 grand opening – because the remote, inaccessible mall was only 20% occupied. At that point, having successfully completed a facility "ahead of schedule" proves vain.

Particularly when it comes to large infrastructure, it might not make much difference whether the "system" is failing to reach its design capacity or that it has delivered capacity or capabilities in excess of what is required at a certain point in time – either scenario will still negatively impact on both operations and financial viability. Indeed, the installed capabilities (whether they be in surplus or in deficit, it might not matter) will not be fully exploited through steady operations to generate sufficient returns to recoup the initial investments (capital outlay) and ensuing maintenance expenditures.

When a certain municipality elected to "build that damn thing once and for all", they ended up delivering a 40 giga-litres water treatment plant, despite indications that the demand would probably remain at around 8.5 giga-litres for the next seven years or so. They deliberately discarded the initial (phased approach) option of installing the plant in four incremental modules of 10 giga-litres to align production throughput to actual demand. But soon after a grand launch, they turned and accused "technical consultants" of misleading the municipality into building the massively oversized facilities; it is now proving costly to operate and maintain "all four 10 giga-litres units", while a single unit would have sufficed given the current demand – a failed "customer demand" readiness.

At the other extreme, the City of Port Elizabeth (South Africa) approved a Bus Rapid Transit (BRT) project in response to increasing pressure on public transport. The BRT was devised to offer a more efficient means of moving passengers and reduce travel time, delay time, and number of stops; it was adopted as an improvement on regular bus services through the combination of features like infrastructure changes in order to provide better operation speeds and reliability. However, the City Press newspaper reported on 26 April 2015 that, six years on, the 60 buses acquired by the

Nelson Mandela Bay Metropolitan Municipality in 2009 for R100 million (to kick-start the BRT system) as part of its "integrated public transport system" were still gathering dust outside a fresh produce market. The same newspaper also wrote that the BRT project, although piloted in 2010, has been plagued by problems and allegations of corruption.

Besides its poor intermodal coordination/network, the BRT system is making use of a median lane configuration (i.e., BRT lane located in the middle of the roadway in a two-way direction), despite a mixed flow traffic lane being problematic. There is no proper shelter for commuters and some pedestrian crossways are not controlled by traffic lights. All these problems have led to the demise of the BRT. "Now this project will never take off and the buses and infrastructure will continue to deteriorate", a local politician said. Even so, later attempts succeeded in reviving the "Libhongolethu" (our pride) BRT system and got it to operate along seven routes despite technical challenges and taxi opposition.

Still, not only were "benefits" delayed for years, but they also proved to be quite inadequate.

The Information and Communications Technology (ICT) as a sector is equally guilty of littering disbenefits to the business community by failing to meet operational targets.

> More often, IT projects fail to achieve most of their intended purpose of increasing productivity, lowering operating costs, improving the quality of work product, and shrinking the time to market … Billions of dollars have been wasted on failed projects [rather than in reducing carbon-footprint[1]], and many highly expensive projects had to be shelved after a short time due to massive resistance from end-users.[2]

Again, the blame for such failures could be placed on a failed or lack of Operational Readiness.

Al-Ahmad proposes a definition of project failure that aligns to Operational Readiness.

> Project failure is defined as any project that is set to support the operations of an organization by exploiting the resources … [but] fails

---

1   The world is preparing to spend trillions of dollars on infrastructure over the next 20 years; but not everyone realises that failure to integrate climate change into the planning of this infrastructure could lead to major adverse and negative development impacts, e.g., crop losses, traffic disruption, reduced power production and higher energy costs.

> to deliver the intended output ... as well as the project comfortably satisfying the stakeholders and being accepted [as non-detrimental to society] and largely used by the end users after deployment.[2]

This stems from the community of end users not being made ready to efficiently operate a "system" or the latter not being safely accommodated in the intended environment.

Operational Readiness is about accommodating both the system and its impacts on the environment.

> Capabilities are exploited in order to achieve outcomes ... [one has] to make some changes in 'business as usual' in order to enable outcomes ... outcomes and benefits are what enable you to achieve transformational corporate objectives ... but [one has to] also recognise that they may lead to dis-benefits [in the operational environment].[18]

In fact, "Business increasingly is seen as a major cause of social, environmental, and economic problems",[48] either by commission or by omission; both business and public sector ought to welcome and promote Operational Readiness.

2 Systems, Systems Engineering and Systems Thinking

Readers who do not need a "refresher" on Systems Engineering may skip this section

When Louis Armstrong sang, "I see trees of green, red roses too. I see them bloom for me and you", perhaps only those who cherish romance could know what the man was really talking about – a fonder heart might not bring about wonders to every soul! For sure, when he got to the stanza that says, "I hear babies crying, I watch them grow. They'll learn much more than I'll never know. And I think to myself what a wonderful world … Yes, I think to myself what a wonderful world", then somebody realised that what one had been taught so far is not all there is to know, nor all there is to be known.

It is amazing what happens to project managers and sponsors when they venture into the world of Systems Thinking and Systems Engineering – what a wonderful world! There is more to be known (beyond what engineering and Project Management have taught us) about how things should work, how to create a world "as it should be" that is as wonderful as "The colors of the rainbow so pretty in the sky", as Armstrong put it. But unlike *babies*, project managers wouldn't cry, though they crave to learn and grow.

If anything, just as ancient navigators used to rely on True North when embarking on a long journey, project managers should perhaps heed the words of Maya Angelou, "Do the best you can until you know better. Then when you know better, do better". Infrastructure and ICT projects are becoming larger and more complex by the day, and Project Management is expected to constantly evolve to remain effective and relevant – academia and practitioners alike are opening a vein of *thinking* and new approaches.

To return to the so-called "practical" world of large-scale projects, Bar-Yam argues that, "A fundamental reason for the difficulties with modern large engineering projects is their inherent complexity. Complexity is generally a characteristic of large engineering projects today".[5] He further remarks that,

> complexity implies that different parts of the system are interdependent so that changes in one part may have effects on other parts of the systems. Complexity may cause unanticipated effects that lead to failures of the system, and in terms of emergent collective behaviours of the system as a whole. Such behaviours are generally difficult to anticipate and understand.[5]

For all this to make sense, one needs to *first* understand what a "system" actually is. A system is defined as

> a construct or collection of different elements that together produce results not obtainable by the elements alone. The elements, or parts, can include people, hardware, software, facilities, policies, and documents; that is, all things required to produce system-level results.[53]

Haskins and Forsberg put it in simple English as follows: "A combination of interacting elements organized to achieve one or more stated purposes". The key words here are "interacting elements", without which this "combination" is reduced to a mere "grouping of things" and, therefore, will not necessary contribute to achieving a common purpose or a set of objectives.[23] From that perspective, both satellites and shopping malls are construed as "systems".

Kossiakoff[32] supports the foregoing definition, as well as its practical implications:

> It was noted previously that the term "system" as commonly used does not correspond to a specific level of aggregation or complexity, it being understood that systems may serve as parts of more complex aggregates or super-systems, and sub-systems may themselves be thought of as systems. For the purpose of the ensuing discussion, this ambiguity will be avoided by limiting the use of the term "system" to those entities that (1) possess the properties of an engineered system, and (2) perform a significant useful service with only the aid of human operators and standard infrastructures (e.g., power grid, highways, fueling stations, and communication lines).

Hence, he further submits, "A passenger aircraft would fit the definition of a system, as would a personal computer with its normal peripherals of input and output keyboard, display, and so on".[32]

Furthermore,

> the complexity of a system is usually determined by the number of
> parts or activities, the degree of differentiation between the parts, and
> the structure of their connections … Complex systems have multi-
> ple interacting components whose collective behaviour cannot be
> simply inferred from the behaviour of the individual components.[21]

Maqsood suggests similarly,

> Construction [and ICT] projects are faced with a challenge that
> must not be underestimated. These projects are increasingly becom-
> ing highly competitive, more complex, and difficult to manage.
> They become problems that are difficult to solve using traditional
> approaches.[35]

It is common cause that modern "man-made" systems (e.g., missiles,
housing estates, bridges) and systems-of-systems (i.e., independently
useful systems incorporated into a larger system that delivers "unique"
capabilities) continually increase in complexity. These systems are being
increasingly developed by partnerships involving multiple suppliers and
developers and often geographically dispersed project teams, involving
several key stakeholders with conflicting concerns and requirements.
There is literally no prospect whatsoever that those systems would ever
get any simpler in the near future.

The International Council on Systems Engineering (INCOSE) has
acknowledged the complex nature of Large Infrastructure Projects (LIPs):

> In LIPs there are many complexities. There may be a number of
> outcomes required by a variety of stakeholders, some seemingly con-
> trary to each other, and many alternative ways to satisfy the require-
> ments all competing for priority and for the same resources and
> finances.[25]

New and systematic Project Management approaches are needed.

So in a paper discussing the application of Systems Engineering (SE)
to building design, Yahiaoui wrote:

> "A more focused use of applying Systems Engineering approach to
> the building design support is presented in response to the ever-
> increasing complexity of buildings. In particular, this paper addresses
> all issues of interrelated dynamic optimisation, as local optimisations

do not give a global optimisation. The paradigm used here is to extend and particularly to adapt the [SE] work carried out in military and space systems to modern building services by taking into account the semantics of buildings in terms of different engineering fields and architecture issues.[59]

SE is therefore an interdisciplinary approach and means to enable the realisation of successful systems. It focuses on defining customer needs and required functionality early in the development cycle, documenting requirements, and then proceeding with design synthesis and system validation while considering the complete problem: operations, schedule and cost, performance, training and support, test, manufacturing, and disposal.[23] "Operations" feature prominently in this definition.

NASA also offers a definition of Systems Engineering that reflects operational needs:

> A disciplined approach for the definition, implementation, integration and operation of a system (product or service) with the emphasis on the satisfaction of stakeholder functional, physical and operational performance requirements in the intended use environment over its planned life cycle within cost and schedule constraints.[53]

The International Council on Systems Engineering (INCOSE) has published a *Guide for the Application of Systems Engineering in Large Infrastructure Projects*. It seeks to reposition the traditional Systems Engineering practices that have been successfully developed and applied on complex projects in the military, aerospace, manufacturing, and telecommunications industries, into the context of the construction industry and thereby provide professionals engaged on Large Infrastructure Projects convenient and comprehensive access to the relevant parts of the system engineer's toolkit.[25]

INCOSE further maintains that,

> the motivation for introducing SE processes on LIPs is a desire to better manage the risks associated with the likely significant degree of change in the environment and associated scope of the project over the extended timescales. Also, the construction process on LIPs can be complex and therefore would benefit from being carefully planned and controlled through implementation using a structured, systematic approach.[25]

This book shares this perspective regarding LIPs.

Moreover, Systems Engineering processes have been retrospectively identified in the construction of ancient megaprojects. Kasser notes, "Depending on their perspective, authors have written that the activities performed in producing the ancient pyramids, the canals and railways of the 19th century and other systems of the past are those embodied in systems engineering".[30] Well, it all started with the pyramids (in Africa)!

The emphasis, however, ought not to have been placed on using Systems Engineering to better perform the construction stage of a project. The focus is on the realisation of the designed (or engineered) solution during construction and the transition into service of the resulting built product, and as a consequence, the application of SE practices is concentrated more on the construction process than on the design of the product or on the continuing operation and maintenance stage [i.e., operability].[25]

One important implication of applying Systems Engineering concepts and principles to enhance Project Lifecycle methodologies entails a lifecycle that reflects an Operational Environment – with the understanding that projects are primarily about improving the particular environment, which extends the responsibility of project teams (thus linking project success) to improvements (or lack thereof) that occur during operations. The whole idea is about starting the project with the end (i.e., improvements in operations) in the mind of the project team – which is a Systems Engineering principle[33,50] (see Figure 2.1).

The above SE principle raises the matter of Operational Readiness into prominence, understanding that, in the first place, projects are initiated for the sake of operations. Hence, another major implication of applying SE concepts to project delivery involves the notion of Verification and Validation (V&V),[23] which INCOSE defines as follows:

(i)   The Verification Process is: "To confirm that all requirements are fulfilled by the system elements and eventual system-of-interest, i.e. that the system has been built right";

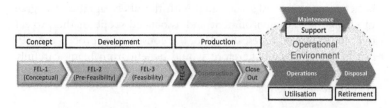

Figure 2.1 Project Lifecycle in accordance with ISO 15288, by the author[33]

(ii) The Validation Process is: "To confirm that the realised system complies with the needs and required functionality of stakeholders, i.e. that the right system has been built".

The Verification and Validation of requirements should indeed take central stage in project delivery because Systems Engineering focuses on managing requirements throughout the Project Lifecycle.[33] This focus (i.e., "It focuses on defining customer needs and required functionality early in the development cycle, documenting requirements") is key to project delivery as "project management is the application of knowledge, skills, tools, and techniques to project activities in order to meet project requirements".[49] For instance, it was said that the requirements for the *ill-fated* space shuttle *Challenger* seemed to be acceptable. But the design, manufacturing, testing, and operation were faulty. Thus, verification was poor – and validation was questionable, because putting schoolteachers and Indian art objects in space does not profit the American taxpayer.

On the other hand, Systems Engineering itself, as a perspective, is based on Systems Thinking, which occurs through discovery, learning, diagnosis, and dialogue that lead to sensing, modelling, and talking about the real world to better understand, define, and work with systems. Further, INCOSE states, Systems Thinking is a unique perspective on reality – a perspective that sharpens our awareness of wholes and how the parts within those wholes interrelate. A systems thinker knows how systems fit into the larger context of day-to-day life, how they behave, and how to manage them.[23]

Many authors would agree with this statement.

> There seems to be a consensus in the literature that you need to apply Systems Thinking to develop solutions to complex problems irrespective of whether you are facing the problems professionally as a trouble-shooter, a systems engineer, a project manager and a diagnostician or if you are facing problems in your personal life, hobby as well as in any other situation.[30]

Still, some authors even offer a mode beyond Systems Thinking.

> While it can help you to understand relationships in situations and think systemically and systematically, Systems Thinking alone cannot help you provide innovative solutions to complex problems … understanding situations is only the first step on the journey that provides those innovative solutions.[30]

Hence, the new approach could be Holistic Thinking!

Holistic Thinking is the combination of analysis, Systems Thinking and critical thinking. Indeed, building on the work of Richmond, Kasser[30] has introduced Holistic Thinking as a set of "viewpoints" on the perspective perimeter called the Holistic Thinking Perspectives. This approach can be used to provide a standard set of anchor points for thinking and communicating in a systemic and systematic manner: "Holistic thinking goes beyond Systems Thinking by not only thinking about a system as a whole but also by doing the thinking in a systemic and systematic manner".[30]

These viewpoints go beyond combining analysis (i.e., internal views) and Systems Thinking (i.e., external views) by adding quantitative and progressive (i.e., temporal, generic, and continuum) viewpoints. In essence, Holistic Thinking as an approach seeks: (1) to separate facts from opinion; and (2) to provides a standard format or template for storing information about situations that facilitates storage and retrieval of information about situations, such as those documented in case studies.[30]

Kasser therefore advocates that "Holistic Thinking" would equip project managers with the requisite skills for creating innovative solutions to modern-day complex problems: The needed skill for providing acceptable solutions is the ability to think differently to that of your contemporaries. You need to go beyond Systems Thinking and apply Holistic Thinking to the matter at hand ... [to devise or deploy successful systems].[30]

Many project practitioners probably started off by studying engineering; they then had to ascend to Systems Thinking, to Systems Engineering, and of late to Holistic Thinking. As complexity increases in Large Infrastructure Projects, so will the need to update our *thinking* regarding project delivery – for "Problems that were created by our current level of thinking cannot be solved by the same level of thinking", as Albert Einstein noted.

Whether this journey will ever end should thus be left for Tantalus (of Greek legend) to tell. Nevertheless, those readers who have already taken baby steps towards Systems Thinking and Systems Engineering and might be crying out for more "learning" should consider consulting INCOSE, NETLIPSE and the Dutch Ministry of Public Works and Water Management for additional information and resources.

3 System Deployment and impacts on environment

System Deployment will involve both the project and the operational environments – addressing the project realm alone (e.g., delivery processes, outputs) would be remiss. Worse still, many project delivery entities focus solely on the "system" to be developed.

In a Systems Engineering (SE) white paper titled, *9 Laws of Effective Systems Engineering*, Scott (2012) stipulates as SE Law No. 9 that Systems Come in 3s: "Every system design involves three systems: The system being designed [i.e., Solution-System], the system it will 'live' in [i.e., Context-System or operational environment], and the system used by the team to design it [i.e., Realisation-System or the project environment]".[50]

Scott (2012) gives the example of designing a subway train, right in the middle of the sketch; to the right of the train is the subway system in which it will operate, and to the left is the process chart depicting the design process (see Figure 3.1).

The Realisation-System is largely discussed in Project Management literature, and it is addressed as part of the Project Management Body of Knowledge (PMBoK and others). This book essentially discusses the processes and challenges of deploying the Solution-System into the Context-System, into its intended operational environment with its impact both on the business/operational and the broader environments.

Martin (2004) has taken the notion of Context-System further in a seminal paper titled, "The Seven Samurai of Systems Engineering: Dealing with the Complexity of 7 Interrelated Systems". He suggests that the Context-System might itself consist of Collaborating-Systems (which collaborate with the deployed system), Sustaining-Systems (which support the operations of the deployed system), and Competing-Systems (which will be vying for resources with the system once deployed).[36] Appreciating these "sub-systems" will enrich the understanding of the Context-System.

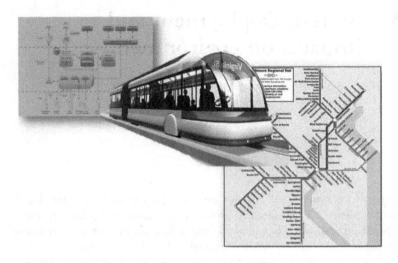

Figure 3.1 Systems come in 3s – Realisation-, Solution-, Context-Systems, as per Scott[50]

Systems are generally designed and developed, and then deployed in order to improve (or establish, in the first place) the intended operational environment, also known as the Context-System. Large Infrastructure Projects (LIPs) in particular are "nested" in the socio-economic environment, and their deployment could entail changes (and sometimes a cascade of changes) in the broader environment that might not necessarily prove positive or beneficial.[14]

"The new system will often change the original Context ... in ways that are sometimes beneficial, but more often ... this change is to the detriment of those we were trying to help", Martin cautions.[36] The essence of Operational Readiness (OR), therefore, is to assure that the system once deployed will operate safely and efficiently, without causing damage to and/or being "impaired" by the adjacent or attendant environment – thus, the deployed system will add value to operations!

It follows that an Operational Readiness process is needed to transition from the project environment (where systems are created and delivered) safely and efficiently to the operational environment (where systems are to be deployed), considering such a deployment might affect both "business/operational" and "broader" environments.

Because the project environment in itself (including the activities therein) is largely temporary, its impact on the broader environment will generally be short term – but practically non-existent vis-à-vis the business/operational environment, except in the case of "brown-field" projects. Most short-term effects on the broader environment usually manifest themselves during the Construction or Production stage; accordingly, they are essentially addressed through the Environmental Impact Assessment (EIA) process – e.g., leading to the Construction Environmental Management process.

On the other hand, following the transition from project to operations, once the system is deployed permanently, long-term effects could be experienced on the business, the operational environment, and the broader environments – and possibly from those environments back onto the deployed system. Many such long-term effects (e.g., radioactive contamination, corrosion or rust, vandalism) will prove near irreversible, even after the eventual Retirement or Disposal of that system.

While long-term effects on the business/operational environment (e.g., staff turnover) will be managed to some extent, controlling long-term negative effects on the broader environment will often prove unattainable. For example, if released into the broader environment, traces of plutonium and certain hydrocarbon wastes take a long time to dissipate or biodegrade, and they may prove severely harmful to species and ecosystems.

Similarly, high levels of heat, humidity, and dust in the operational environment would cause damage to delicate subsystems (e.g., electronics, plasma display units) – unless mitigating mechanisms (e.g., anti-corrosion, air-conditioning, dust-filtering) are put in place and sustained throughout the lifespan of operations (i.e., Utilisation Phase)[52] (see Figure 3.2).

The impacts of System Deployment on the operational and broader environments are particularly manifest in large-scale infrastructure projects (e.g., pollution, destruction of species and ecologies, exacerbation of social ills) and are only ignored at the peril of the unsuspecting public to whom the "burden" of detrimental effects will be shifted.[38] Hence, their business case ought to reflect any negative socio-economic externalities.

Above all, from a System Thinking perspective, due consideration should be given as to how the project intervention might affect other systems/subsystems in connected ecologies. The *Los Angeles Times* of 8 April 2019 wrote, "The Ethiopians are building a massive dam, and Egypt is worried" – a case of socio-economic externalities in action! The construction of Africa's biggest hydroelectric dam could also bring a "man-made" calamity to one of its biggest economies, miles away from the host country of Ethiopia.

The US$ 4-billion Grand Ethiopian Renaissance Dam (GERD) is set to be the biggest hydropower plant in Africa – and is being hailed

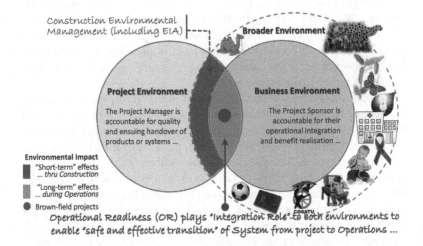

Figure 3.2 Project, business/operational, and broader environments

as a national achievement, "as big as Aswan High Dam in Egypt was in the 1960s"; but Egypt would not take kindly to such an *insensitive* comparison. Since Ethiopia announced plans nearly a decade ago to build a massive hydroelectric dam along the Blue Nile tributary, the Egyptian government has waited in dread at the catastrophic prospects that its Nile freshwater lifeline could slow by as much as 25%.

> "We don't have any other resource in Egypt except the Nile water", warned Professor Nader Nour el-Din (soil and water expert at Cairo University, Egypt) – "This will harm Egypt!".

Since the Nile runs the length of the country from its southern border with Sudan north into the Mediterranean Sea, the "sacred" river provides more than 90% of Egypt's freshwater. So during a news conference in Cairo, the Ethiopian prime minister promised Egyptians, "I swear to God, we will never hurt you", after the Egyptian president, Abdel Fattah Sisi, pressed him to swear in front of the Egyptian people that he would not harm the country's Nile water share. Egyptian officials have sought to scuttle or minimise the negative impact of the planned 6,450-megawatt facility, with Ethiopia planning to fill it in 3 years and Egypt instead asking for 15 years "to better prepare for the future"!

This proves beyond doubt that as a result of project scope/activities, adverse impacts could arise in attendant "systems" – but this need not necessarily be in proximity of space or time. While the completion of the Grand Ethiopian Renaissance Dam is set to provide electricity to the 60% of Ethiopia's population that have no access, it will *similarly* disrupt the freshwater supply downstream in the fertile strip along the Nile for farming and water – though the doomsday event will only take place in 3 to 15 years. Currently, 95% of Egypt's population reside in the Nile Valley; a set of adverse impacts may befall them, even though Ethiopia never intended to burden Egypt with disbenefits – but merely expected to reap countless socio-economic benefits from the dam (hence, "Renaissance").

The ambit of Operational Readiness stretches beyond the *immediate* environment and should include the collaborating, sustaining, or competing systems/subsystems *elsewhere* as relevant.

In fact, the "Network for the Dissemination of Knowledge on the Management and Organisation of Large Infrastructure Projects in Europe" (NETLIPSE) reviewed 15 large-scale projects across Europe and accordingly published the NETLIPSE Report.[44] Findings concerning the impacts of large-scale projects on the "environment" included:

- It appears that LIPs in Europe share similar characteristics. The projects are not only large scale and complex, but also have a major impact on the environment [beyond its direct vicinity]. The period of inception until realisation often covers decades; new technologies and legislation are developed and introduced in the project; the projects have immense budgets, often billions of Euros; and many stakeholders are involved. It is no wonder then that the scope of a[n] LIP changes through time. All these characteristics present the project's management [e.g., its business case] with diverse challenges often resulting in time or cost overruns;

- It has also become clear that the effectiveness of Project Management and organisation does not only depend upon these factors within the direct control of project managers. Projects have to be realised in a dynamic and multiple context. Context factors also have an impact on the realisation of projects which may be decisive. This means that the effective project delivery organisation also has to deal with factors that may stretch beyond a projects' boundary [i.e., into adjacent systems], therefore also emphasizing the importance of "openness" in projects;

- LIPs have a "non-linear" development of the implementation process [i.e., minor changes may cause major effects] ... As mentioned, external context factors have a decisive influence on their development. We believe that [minor] unexpected or changing conditions, for instance new legislation on fire regulation in tunnels or on safety systems on railway lines, will always occur and will impact projects.

Moreover, referring to one of these 15 projects, the NETLIPSE Report remarked,

> independent experts have confirmed that in general the standard of final design and of construction has been high. The project involved limited technical innovation – the Viedenská to Pristavny Most section of road was coated in an environmentally friendly form of asphalting as part of an EU sponsored trial ... this material has reduced noise levels and more efficient run-off and drainage of surface water. However careful monitoring of the special maintenance regime that is required to determine whether there will be any increase in whole life costs.

It thus confirms that besides design and construction, project delivery shall address "impacts" on the surrounding environment.

Depending on the nature and scale of the infrastructure project, adverse impacts and risks to the surrounding environment can be many and diverse, including the following:

(I)   During the Construction phase:

- Loss of land and/or natural resources that are important to local livelihoods;
- Deterioration of surface water bodies (e.g., wetlands, springs, brooks, rivers);
- Damage to road (due to construction traffic), water and health infrastructure;
- Conflicts between the native population and the "hired" migrant workforce;
- Heightened risks of communicable disease due to the influx of migrant workers;
- Loss of habitat and wildlife disturbances due to the sourcing of building materials;
- Nuisances and other health concerns from heavy traffic (e.g., construction trucks to/from site), dust, noise, excessive lighting, and noxious air emissions.

Then again, the same Construction period is also perceived by many stakeholders as an opportunity to secure anticipated local economic benefits, whether through favourable compensation arrangements, direct or indirect (part-time) employment opportunities, using temporary construction works to support local infrastructure development, or, in the case of larger projects, dedicated community development programmes (e.g., a clinic).

(II) During the Operations phase:

- Community health, safety, hazards, and risks due to activities of operations;
- Environmental and ecological damages due to wastes/"effluents" disposal;
- Re-employment prospects for workers deserting other trades (e.g., farming);
- Potential to cause a public emergency – explosion, hazardous spills, flooding.

At the eventual Disposal, commensurate with the scale of potential environmental or socio-economic impacts and risks, the project team might wish to consider producing regular reports, targeted at the affected stakeholders, which outline progress against agreed plans and which focus on issues of greatest concern to the residents including:

- Compensation benefits and re-employment opportunities in (other) trades;
- Training/local enterprise support for economic re-integration/conversion;
- Environmental/ecological rehabilitation following asset decommissioning;
- Progress in the transfer of physical assets/lands to other owners or users;
- Future status of bulk services and infrastructure following assets disposal.

4   Necessity of Operational Readiness

System Deployment is completed during the Transition Process and Start-Up is an integral part of it.

> Ultimately, the Transition Process transfers custody of the system and responsibility for system support from one organizational entity to another. This includes, but is not limited to, transfer of custody from the development team to the organizations that will subsequently operate and support the system. Successful conclusion of the Transition Process typically marks the beginning of the Utilization Stage of the system-of-interest.[23,20]

The responsibility to *"operate and support"* still stands!

The International Council on Systems Engineering (INCOSE) further cautions,

> while this is a relatively short process, it should be carefully planned to avoid surprises and recrimination on either side of the agreement. Additionally, transition plans should be tracked and monitored to ensure all activities are completed to both parties' satisfaction, including resolution of any issues arising during transition.[23]

This is crucial in turnkey projects where the owner-organisation is often expected to play a passive role during delivery, but still be ready for operations.

In fact, GP Strategies (a global company based in the USA) maintains that,

> a key goal of capital projects is to achieve a State of Operational Readiness in order to achieve successful Start-Up on time and within budget ... Another goal is to reach a State of Operational Excellence as soon as possible after Start-Up.[22,24]

Unless it improves operations, project delivery would be in vain; benefits realisation (or strategy) will not happen except through improved operations.

For example, as a "terminal-system", the £4.3 billion London (UK) Heathrow Airport Terminal 5 (T5) has been acknowledged as the "most successful UK construction project" owing to the innovative Project Management practices used, which focused on collaboration (around constructability, not much on operability).[9] It was hailed as "British Airways' most technologically advanced and lavish terminal in the world"[24] – T5 is Europe's largest free-standing structure and was also keenly anticipated by travellers and British Airway alike, "And it's an impressive building", one should add.[52]

However, Bourne (2010) remarks that although T5 was officially opened on 14 March 2008 by HM Queen Elizabeth it only began operating on 27 March 2008 – any red flag? From the first day flights had to be cancelled, passengers were stranded, and over 15 000 pieces of baggage were lost.[9] "We had all believed genuinely that it would be a great opening, which clearly it wasn't", the then-airport chairman moaned.[52]

Bourne[9] further notes that an enquiry was ordered by the House of Commons Transport Committee. The report released (same year) included the following findings:

- Baggage handlers claimed that they had not been adequately trained and did not have any support or backup even on the first day;
- British Airways (BA) asked for volunteers to make up additional numbers to provide this support, but due to low morale staff were not prepared to attend on their day off;
- Staff did not know what tasks they had to perform on the opening day;
- Check-in staff continued to add bags to the system, causing the new baggage handling system to overload, because baggage handlers were not removing them quickly enough off the belts. There was no over-ride switch to stop the belts.

The report clearly indicated that T5 had not attained Operational Readiness on its 14 March opening. This embarrassing mistake was avoided years later when Heathrow Airport upgraded and refurbished its Terminal 2 (T2). A dedicated company was hired around 2013 to manage the Operational Readiness process on the terminal. As a result, when HM Queen Elizabeth opened T2 on 23 June 2014, the transition to operations went much more smoothly.

The Heathrow Airside Operational Readiness (OR) Manager thus noted, "[*Company's name concealed*] have comprehensibly tested the operability of T2's most critical passenger sensitive piece of equipment – the air bridges and stand design ... the significance of this success story cannot be underestimated".[10] Well, it has saved the Queen another embarrassment!

Further, the Head of Terminal Operations and Passenger Experience (Terminal 2) claimed.[10]

> The work has consistently been referred to in the highest standards by those benefiting from it. In particular, the work done around check-in processes and creating a "users guide" ... has been identified as the [OR] "blueprint" for how to get things done.

As was the case with Heathrow Airport, many organisations spend billions on capital projects to build, expand, and upgrade infrastructure systems and other assets or facilities with the expectation of attaining improvements in their current operations – which should translate into better services and/or higher shareholder returns and, ultimately, help the host country increase its wealth and its citizens' standard of living. These socio-economic returns only accrue when the project is delivered satisfactorily.

While those megaprojects might get completed on time, on budget, and to technical specifications, many such infrastructure systems still struggle and/or fail to add value owing to, inter alia, the fact that the owner's environment "was not made adequately ready to safely receive and efficiently operate the newly-built system, asset or facility". Moreover, recent studies (e.g., Deloitte & Touche[12]) have revealed the following:

(i)   Retrofitting Operational Readiness may cost the owner-organisation up to an additional 25% of the Estimated Total Costs, and will cause the project to fail.[41] However, it usually costs far less (±4%) when planned-in from the project onset;

(ii) Failure or lack of Operational Readiness may cause up to 30% loss of returns due to delayed and/or ailing Ramp-Up, which has the potential to defeat the viability of the business case.

Merrow (2011) argues that failure (due to poor Front-End-Loading, FEL) of the project to produce at or near the rates that were promised at project approval (i.e., Vertical Ramp-Up) is debilitating to the economics of the project (e.g., NPV, IRR, ROI, ROCE).

If product prices remain constant, the early years' production are the most valuable the project will ever have. It follows that operability failure in early years (e.g., slow, delayed, or ailing Ramp-Up) could cause bankruptcy or a "fire sale" of company assets[41] (see Figure 4.1).

Operability failures (e.g., erratic operations, inconsistent production) will often cause operating costs to escalate, resulting in operating profits and/or quality of products and/or services noticeably decreasing. This predicament is exacerbated when safety performance deteriorates to the extent of impairing operations (e.g., persistent breakdowns) or causing occupational injuries and fatalities, leading to its "shutdown".

Slow and erratic Ramp-Up are bad for business and may jeopardise the project's NPV and the company's ROCE and reputation. Operations are generally expected to reach 90% of the Design Capacity at Start-Up (refer to Figure 4.1), and the investment in OR could often be the differentiator – across human elements, technology (e.g., equipment, tools), and processes. Further, even well-designed support-systems will need strong and specific foundations so as to facilitate a viable "Vertical Start-Up". The next example shows that "flawed foundations" may lead to failed System Deployment.

Waste Management, Inc. was a leading provider of waste and environmental services in North America. They once executed a so-called "out-of-the-box" ERP (i.e., Enterprise Resource Planning) project without implementing Operational Readiness and suffered substantial financial loss as a result; project costs were not recouped, benefits were not realised, and ROCE deteriorated.

The whole debacle surfaced in 2008 when

Waste Management announced that it was suing SAP ... over the failure of an ERP implementation ... Waste Management said that

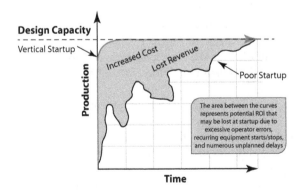

Figure 4.1 Vertical Start-Up versus Poor Start-Up, as per GP Strategies[22]

it was seeking the recovery of more than $100 million in project expenses as well as "the savings and benefits that the SAP software was promised to deliver to Waste Management" … according to Waste Management, "Almost immediately following execution of the agreements, the SAP implementation team discovered significant 'gaps' between the software's functionality and Waste Management's business requirements" … But members of SAP's implementation team had reportedly blamed Waste Management for the functional gaps [i.e., flawed foundations] and had submitted change orders requiring that Waste Management pay for fixing them.[52]

Operational Readiness is a Project Lifecycle imperative. It proves most effective when embedded (rather than appended) in the Project Lifecycle methodology. Thankfully, those vital lessons learned at Heathrow Airport between T5 and T2 terminals were made available to Dubai Airports[52] and are now accessible to any organisation willing to harness Operational Readiness in order to secure a successful System Deployment.

The necessity for Operational Readiness arises from the experiential repercussions of its failure, such as those illustrated in the examples of the Heathrow Terminal T5 and the Waste Management against SAP debacles. From a Systems Engineering perspective, and based on the work of Scott,[50] the "interface" between the Solution-System and the Context-System is the preserve of Operational Readiness, the space of transitioning from the project to the operations realm. This interface has to be managed for the system (or rather system-of-systems, SoS) to perform as such.

This is an essential task of the System Engineer, according to the NASA *Handbook of SE*.

The systems engineer will usually play the key role in leading the development of the system architecture, defining and allocating requirements, evaluating design tradeoffs, balancing technical risk between systems, defining and assessing interfaces, providing oversight of verification and validation activities, as well as many other tasks.[53]

It is important to define all interface requirements for the system, including those to enabling systems [i.e., Context-System]. The external interfaces form the boundaries between the product and the rest of the world. Types of interfaces include operational command and control, computer to computer, mechanical, electrical, thermal, and data. One useful tool in defining interfaces is the context diagram …, which depicts the product and all of its external interfaces.

Once the product components are defined, a block diagram showing the major components, interconnections, and external interfaces of the system should be developed to define both the components and their interactions.[53]

Operational Readiness essentially "enables" better system operation.

The INCOSE *SE Handbook*[20] warns that, "Unless someone defines and controls the scope of a SoS and manages the boundaries of system elements, no one controls the definition of the external interfaces". Fuzzy boundaries (e.g., not being sure whether the newly deployed system will fit into or operate in the intended environment) cause confusion and undermine system performance. Thus, INCOSE further states, "Focus is placed on controlling the interfaces between system elements and external systems".[20] These external interfaces include "functional and design interfaces to interacting systems, platforms, and/or humans external to the system boundary".[20] Operational Readiness is needed to "Identify [and manage] interfaces between system elements and with external and enabling systems", which is crucial in defining the "architecture" of the system, and any changes required in the intended environment.

> To achieve good results, systems engineers involve themselves in nearly every aspect of a project [Operational Readiness], pay close attention to interfaces where two or more systems or system elements work together, and establish an interaction network with stakeholders and other organizational units of the enterprise [architecture].[20]

Further, these

> these technical processes [of SE Transition Management] enable systems engineers to coordinate the interactions between engineering specialists, systems stakeholders and operators, and manufacturing. They also address conformance with the expectations and legislated requirements of society. These processes lead to the creation of a full set of requirements that address the desired capabilities within the bounds of performance, environment, external interfaces, and design constraints.[20]

Slack[52] makes an *insightful* comment: "Design becomes particularly important at the interface between products or services and the people that use [or operate] them".[52]

Operational Readiness is, thus, about integrating the newly designed system into its intended environment, assuring that it will prove safe and efficient once deployed in operations. Now, INCOSE takes an "operational view" of System Integration as follows:

> The Integration Process includes activities to acquire or design and build enabling systems needed to support the integration of system elements and demonstration of end-to-end operation. This process confirms all boundaries between system elements have been correctly identified and described, including physical, logical, and human-system interfaces; and confirms that all functional, performance, and design requirements and constraints are satisfied. Interim assembly configurations are tested to assure correct flow of information and data across interfaces to reduce risk, and minimize errors and time spent isolating and correcting them.[20]

Hence, during a series of structured interviews with Subject Matter Experts (SMEs) and mature project practitioners in 2005, the author[33] proceeded to discuss the rationale of considering operational input into the Front End Planning of Large Infrastructure Projects (LIPs). The following "Operational Readiness" responses were then recorded:

(I)   *"There is a need to think strategically about operations, maintenance and disposal right from the beginning and propose system-solutions accordingly"* – Operational Readiness is needed!

(II)   *"Failure to do so might lead to the delivering of a new asset, but not necessarily a workable business solution"* – Operational Readiness is a business imperative!

5 Scope of Operational Readiness

Forsberg has eloquently discussed the Denver Airport from an Operational Readiness perspective. He noted,

> Even though baggage handling is a key part of any airport, the Denver Airport state-of-the-art baggage handling system was an afterthought not factored into the concept, the architecture, or the operating scenarios. The system had to be designed and installed within the inadequate physical constraints of existing designs and operations already under construction; these constraints prohibited an effective backup system.[19]

A critical "operational component" of any functional airport was treated as an afterthought, possibly due to a lack of an adequate framework!

This oversight had major adverse operational repercussions, even as Forsberg further deplores:

> Unfortunately, the approved Denver Airport plan was never re-baselined to accommodate the add-on baggage handling capability as it should have been. As a result, the costs soared from $1.7 billion to more than $4.8 billion, a [massive] ± 200% overrun, and the operational readiness was delayed 16 months; its business case has failed, since the higher levels of bonded debt would require approximately $2 billion in additional interest payments.[19]

This predicament was of course bad for airport operations, and business, and the long-term viability of the owner organisation.

Unless adequate Operational Readiness (OR) Planning is undertaken, the project team may fail to correctly define the "scope" (i.e., intervention areas), their costs, and the optimal timelines of Operational Readiness Implementation. This would defeat the value and benefits that the particular project is expected to deliver, based on its business case. Thus, it is worth noting that all other delivery parameters do flow from the "scope".[49]

Of equally great significance is the inference (by the author) from the seminal work of Martin (2008)[36] that the Context-System (which shares most of the characteristics of complexity and architecture with the Realisation-System) should in theory encompass the following technical and organisational components: (1) people and organisations; (2) facilities and equipment; (3) materials and supplies; (4) services and utilities; (5) processes and methods; (6) tools and techniques; (7) policies and procedures; (8) data and information; and (9) knowledge and wisdom.

For practical reasons, however, these components (the "scope") will be reduced to four essential Organisational Domains for Operational Readiness Requirements as follows:

(1) Legal and Statutory Requirements (e.g., licensing and permitting, compliance);
(2) Human Resources Requirements (e.g., skills, culture, structures, interactions);
(3) Processes Requirements (e.g., workflows, ICT transactional/operating systems);
(4) Utilities/Infrastructure Requirements (e.g., bulk services, facilities, logistics).

Moreover, Operational Readiness Requirements should consider the needs and demands of the Competing, Collaborative, and Sustaining systems within the intended operational environment[36] – as well as commercial and contractual considerations, i.e., "Is there a market available and made ready for the new system to be deployed?". For example, the initiators of the Iridium Project neglected its commercial aspects at their own peril; facing bankruptcy, they sold a promising venture at 2% of the capital outlay and somebody else reaped the reward of its lucrative commercialisation.[19,20]

In another instance that illustrates the importance of sorting out "commercial" issues from the start, newly completed homes at the Dube Housing Project (Soweto, South Africa) went protractedly unoccupied and ended up being vandalised and looted when beneficiaries disagreed with government over allocation modalities (e.g., Who is on the official list? Are houses freehold or leasehold? At what price? Will title deeds be issued?). No "system" is deemed completed unless it is successfully deployed in its intended operational environment; a lesson the Dube

Table 5.1 Operational Readiness challenges and impacts on operations

Operational Readiness challenges	Possible impacts on operations
Legal and Statutory Readiness: *Securing licences to operate or applying for new byelaws to allow/ protect operations*	• Delayed Start-Up to allow legal process • Waste Disposal prohibited/riot allowed • Operations halted for non-compliance
Human Resources Readiness: *Addressing skills and capacity shortages or organisational design flaws*	• Increased costs due to "imported" skills • Confused roles and responsibilities • Suboptimal production throughput • Poor quality and/or safety records
Processes/Systems Readiness: *Ensuring workflows and related management systems (including ICT platform, ERP) are able to support changes in operating environment*	• Constrained management effectiveness • Inability to produce meaningful reports for management and other stakeholders • Material and critical parts shortage
Services and Infrastructure Readiness: *Availability of infrastructure and related services and supplies to support operations*	• Operations hampered by lack of supply • Increased production costs due to *pro tem* supplies (e.g., by use of generator) • Delay/inability to reach design capacity
Commercial Agreement: *Signing Off-take Agreements before start-up*	• Lack of customers for products/services • Customer(s) not ready/able to transact

project manager learnt the hard way! Table 5.1 reflects a number of possible implications of OR failure.

Addressing the above readiness considerations should never be taken for granted, otherwise they will stand in the way of benefits realisation – and many organisations have now learned this the hard way. Nobody wants an oil refinery that cannot reach its optimum capacity due to inadequate or erratic power supply. By way of illustration, Figure 5.1 reflects a number of considerations related to System Utilisation Readiness (based on sustainability, operability, maintainability, availability, reliability – SOMAR).

Project outputs ought to be utilised (i.e., in "improved operations", or else nothing) for organisational strategy to be realised. Indeed, ISO 21500 stipulates that,

> Selected opportunities are further developed in a business case ... and can result in one or more projects that provide deliverables. Those deliverables can be used [i.e. operated, maintained, and disposed of] to realize benefits. The benefits can be an input to realize and further the organizational strategy.[27]

Primary OR Domain	OR Domain's Aspects	OR Domain Considerations, as per Operating Model
Human Resources	Training & Skills Transfer	*New skills required? For whom? Skill Provision Scheme?*
	Human Resources Capacity	*New recruits required? By when?*
	Organisational Change Management	*Any changes to Structure (and office space) or Culture?*
Operational Support	Bulk Supply/Services & Utilities	*New, extra Water/Electricity Supply, Sewerage needed?*
	Logistics, Supply Chain Management	*Wherewithal to procure/dispatch goods, services needed?*
	Customer/Commercial agreements	*Are off-take contracts in place for end-products/services?*
	Financials (Δ Working Capital, Budget)	*Additional funds needed to support "added" operations?*
	Configuration Management	*How to maintain current & accurate versions of data?*
	SOMAR – *ilities*	*Any set-up to allow system to operate in its environment?*
System/Prod Utilisation	Operational Health & Safety & Security	*What HSS, Continuity regimen needed for safe utilisation?*
	Operational Licencing & Permitting	*Any Operating Licence, Waste Disposal Permit needed?*
	Technology Integration & ICT platforms	*How to align ERP, other systems to new load/technology?*
	System/Product Testing	*What testing process, equipment & components needed?*
Facilities & Tools (considering property & facilities management)	Operations Facilities	*Facilities, equipment, F&F, tie-ins needed for operations?*
	Spare Parts and/or Components	*Any spares, feedstock needed for testing, for operations?*
	Maintenance Facilities and Equipment	*Any facilities, plants, equipment needed for maintenance?*
Processes & Procedures	Maintenance Regime & Plans	*What types, scope, budget and timing of maintenance?*
	Operational Risk Management	*What operational risks to mitigate? Manuals needed?*
	Warrantees Management	*What types, scope & processes? Whose responsibility?*

Figure 5.1 Extract from Operational Readiness (OR) Considerations

Further, a particular attention ought to be drawn to Legal and Statutory Readiness – and its related requirements. While legal matters might not (positively or otherwise) "physically" contribute to operations, they are significant in delineating the legal (and socially acceptable) "universe" within which such operations should take place. Indeed, formal "legal consents"[44] are markedly essential due to large-scale systems (e.g., Large Infrastructure Projects, LIPs) being technological systems that are "nested" in the socio-economic environment.[14]

As such, Legal and Statutory Readiness informs the legality (and social acceptability) of every other domain of Operational Readiness, including Human Resources (e.g., labour law and practices), Processes (e.g., occupational health, hazardous waste bills), Utilities and Infrastructure (e.g., provision of public services treated as a constitutional obligation[14,44])[1], and Commercial Agreements (e.g., legality of contracts with suppliers).

Legal and Statutory Readiness, thus, not only indirectly impacts every other readiness domain, but also has the potential to cause or justify an "administrative shutdown" of operations by the relevant authorities,

---

1 In many developing countries, "leftist/socialistic" policies will likely impose limits on the tariff and use of land, water, or electricity – whereas "advanced" economies will invoke "eminent domain" (US) or "compulsory purchase" (UK) clauses over a land.

should the activities or outcomes of operations be perceived as being illegal and/or socially undesirable.

This concern could even apply to the Solution-System itself, as a way of preventing it from damaging the environment. This may involve a certification process, requiring a "Written assurance [by the right agency] that the product ... has been developed and can perform its assigned functions in accordance with legal or industrial standards".[23]

Another aspect of compliance, albeit softer, pertains to the notion of Corporate Social Responsibility (CSR).

> It is increasingly recognized by many businesses that operations managers have a set of broad societal responsibilities and concerns beyond their direct activities. The general term for these aspects of business responsibility is "corporate social responsibility" ... It should be of particular interest to operations managers, because their activities can have a direct and significant effect on society.[52]

Citing UK government sources, Slack observes that,

> CSR is the business contribution to our sustainable development goals ... it is about how business takes account of its economic, social and environmental impacts in the way it operates – maximizing the benefits and minimizing the downsides ... we see CSR as the voluntary actions that business can take, over and above compliance with minimum legal requirements, to address both its own competitive interests and the interests of wider society...[52]

so as to avert the "Tragedy of the Commons" where "Every user benefits directly from its [shared resources'] use, but shares the costs of its abuse with everyone else".[38]

Citing the World Business Council for Sustainable Development, Slack further stresses CSR is "The continuing commitment by business to behave ethically and contribute to economic development while improving [not ruin] the quality of life of the workforce and their families as well as of the local community and society at large".[52]

The *Urbis et Orbit* motto (i.e., to the city and to the world; thus, to the system itself and to the environment) shall apply here; Operational Readiness Requirements should aim at ensuring the deployed Solution-System not only performs effectively in its intended environment, but does so without causing harm or damage to itself, to the owner organisation, nor to its operating and/or broader environments where it lives.

The above arguments, again, attest that the whole purpose of Operational Readiness should not only be about accommodating the Solution-System once deployed in the intended operational environment, but also about preserving the adjacent business, operational and broader environments where it operates. Further, system operations should, of necessity, maintain such a readiness over the lifecycle, not just at Ramp-Up.

> Long-term system success and customer satisfaction rely heavily upon demonstrated effectiveness of the total [i.e., operationally-devised] system inclusive of its decision-makers, operators, maintainers, supported customers, sustainers, and the support network. In all systems, failure to address long-term, life-cycle issues can result in failure to achieve the intended purpose/mission, a poor design, unnecessary burdens [and stress] on the workers, increased incidence of human errors, excessive total cost of ownership, and, in some cases, negative impacts to the environment and public health and safety. Additionally, economic consequences may include lost customer confidence, lost market share, product liability, and little repeat business. Without this total system approach [i.e., Concept of Operations], the system as an enterprise solution will not meet optimal total system performance and/or total cost of ownership objectives.[23]

Therefore, the relevance of OR Requirements flows from the Concept of Operations (ConOps).

It is the envisaged Concept of Operations (or "day-in-the-life" of the Solution-System to be deployed in operations) that governs the Operational Readiness Scope. As such, Operational Readiness prepares the operational environment to accommodate a safe and efficient utilisation of the Solution-System, whether as infrastructure, computer systems (ICT), or both. And the industry is witnessing a growing convergence between ICT and infrastructure; computer systems are now widely used in mines, factories, railways, and roads.

This is but a straightforward exercise, especially in "brown-field" projects whereby the Concept of Operations itself might undergo alterations. There will often arise the need to sustain the existing operations (to maintain the business as a going concern), while ramping up the new "system", and concomitantly retiring the old (or redundant) operational arrangements.[18] For that reason, Operational Readiness Requirements

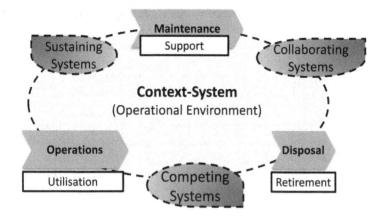

Figure 5.2 Context-System, by the author[33]

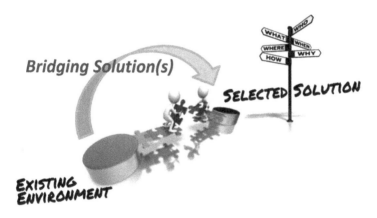

Figure 5.3 Transition to Operations, adapted from BA Experts[3]

(for "Operability") will emanate from two important project delivery areas as follows:

(1) The Context-System (where the new system will be deployed, as per the ConOps) – Operational Requirements are "changes" to current/planned state of Operations (see Figure 5.2).

These "adjustment" requirement items arise from consultations with stakeholders and shall also include the changes to Operational Environment that will enable a "smooth transition" at Ramp-Up and Operational Excellence after Start-Up – e.g., what changes are needed in Collaborating systems to allow safe Operations and eventual Disposal?

(2) Transition Mode (to support the new "Solution-System", while it is being deployed) – Transition Requirements include any "interim arrangements" in the Realisation-System (e.g., EPC/M, Contractors), in the Context-System, or in the Solution itself (see Figure 5.3).

Those "bridging" requirement items (also applicable to Disposal of "As Is") include backups, interfaces, technical support staff, workflow designs, process models, database conversions, bypasses and over-rides, job descriptions, and training and capacitation. Hence, "An organization also requires sufficient financial capital to fund its [increased] ... operating expenses"[6] – which here may entail an "injection" of working capital.[52]

6 Operational Readiness and Project Lifecycle

Systems Engineering practices such as Transition Management and Asset Lifecycle considerations can be embedded onto Project Lifecycle methodologies to improve the management of the system's requirements throughout the lifecycle, from concept to operations to its eventual disposal. This is a further step in the right direction of parting with the frequent, pernicious "rush to get the substance of the project under way".[40]

Successful delivery of capital/infrastructure projects ultimately relies on the extent of their readiness to transition into operations due to a tendency of any newly deployed system to not only rely on, but also impact on or be impaired by its environment (as a Complex-Adaptive-System, CAS). Any robust Project Lifecycle methodology (PLM) will, thus, fittingly accommodate a "built-in" Operational Readiness (OR) process.[33,49]

The author argues that project delivery shall start with new/improved operations (i.e., the end) in mind. Therefore, Operational Readiness ought not to be an afterthought – but an afterthought process.

According to the Independent Project Analysts (IPA), global data on megaprojects delivery reveal that

> There is a [fairly strong] relationship between the incidence of Operability Failure and the FEL; when the level of FEL is "good" or better, the number of operability failures is reduced to an acceptable level, but as soon as FEL index moves into the "fair" range, operability collapses.[41]

Inadequate FEL breeds poor operability.

It is so ironic that many teams will literally rush FEL processes (and ignore key readiness requirements, e.g., licence, feedstock, tie-ins) in a bid to get operations started sooner!

Operational Readiness is supposed to "materialise" from the point where the system transitions from the project to the operational environment. However, because of its strong coupling to FEL phases, it will be sensible to build up such a readiness (i.e., OR planning) from project onset. Awareness of readiness should be maintained through the system development lifecycle (SDLC). Involving all key stakeholders throughout the lifecycle is one approach to improve the chances of a successful System Deployment.

For instance, establishing both the current OR baseline (i.e., "As Is") and the High-Level Operational Readiness Requirements ("Should Be", based on the selected ConOps) at the Conceptual Phase would not only make sense, but would also conform to the lifecycle principle of progressive elaboration,[33] although the detailed Operational Readiness Plan would only be available near the start of Production/Execution phases.

The physical facility is like the tip of an iceberg: Operational Readiness (its bottom part) should be developed along with the "system", for retrofitting of OR is costly and risky (see Figure 6.1).

Table 6.1 provides a synopsis of OR Activities and Deliverables over the Project Lifecycle, starting with high-level OR Requirements to evolve into a "detailed" OR Plan. It indicates that a detailed OR Plan reflecting risks and financial (i.e., budget) and timeline (i.e., schedule) implications are required at Feasibility phase (or Front End Loading phase 3, FEL-3). Both budget and schedule ought to be incorporated into the business case to be approved at that stage. Further, off-take agreements should be "accepted" at FEL-3 to ensure that the project is approved

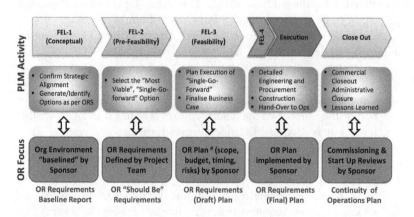

Figure 6.1 OR Requirements per generic Project Lifecycle phase

Table 6.1 Progressive elaboration of OR Activities and Deliverables

Project phase	Operational Readiness (OR) Activities	OR Deliverables/Outcomes
FEL-1	• Project Sponsor provides Operating Model (i.e., High-Level, Current and Should Be) to Project Team • Project Sponsor provides Business Impact & Business Benefits (Macro-Level) to the Project Team • Project Manager develops High-Level OR Requirements (including Maintenance & Disposal needs) • Project Manager develops/compiles OR Baseline (i.e., "As Is" in line with OR Elements) in conjunction with Project Sponsor	• OR Baseline (i.e. "As Is" in line with OR Elements) • OR High-Level Requirements in line with relevant OR Elements, as per Operating Model (ConOps) and projected "Carrying Capacity"
FEL-2	• Project Sponsor provides Detailed Operating Model (and/or Operational Risks) to Project Team • Project Manager provides Detailed OR Requirements (i.e., "Should Be") as per relevant OR Elements • Project Sponsor determines OR Gaps in line with relevant OR Elements • Project Sponsor provides High-Level Costs and Schedule Implications of OR Requirements • OR Costs may entail CAPEX – what requires CAPEX (e.g., facility) should be incorporated in Scope	• "Should Be" OR Requirements per option as per OR Elements • High Level OR Costs & Schedule Implications per option in line with relevant OR Elements
FEL-3	• Project Sponsor develops/prepares Draft OR Plan (e.g., including OR scope, Costs, Schedule, Risks, Roles & Responsibilities) to be carried out during the "Execution" Phase – and "Off-take" Agreements • Project Manager reflects the essence of Draft OR Plan in the following: a) Business and Operational Case (e.g., Costs, Ramp-Up Schedule, and Risks); b) Feasibility Report (e.g., Scope and Risks); c) Project Execution Plan (e.g., Scope integrated with Project Works, Costs, Schedule, and Risks)	• Draft OR Plan (e.g., OR Scope, Costs, Schedule, Risks, and Roles & Responsibilities), which will be implemented by Project Sponsor during ensuing "Execution Phase" • Detailed OR Costs & Schedule for selected option are approved

(Continued)

Table 6.1 Continued

Project phase	Operational Readiness (OR) Activities	OR Deliverables / Outcomes
FEL-4	• Permitting and Licensing – requirements ascertained, applications lodged (to be granted by FEL-4) • Project Sponsor and Project Manager to review and finalise OR outcomes of preceding FEL-3 • Commercial agreements (e.g., Off-take Agreements, Feedstock & Supply Contracts) finalised, signed	• "Off-take" Agreements approved • Revised OR Costs & Schedule • Signed-off OR Plan & Agreements
Construction	Project Sponsor (or OR Manager) to implement/carry out Final OR Plan in collaboration/conjunction with implementation of Project Execution Plan (PEP) by Project Manager	Milestones/Final OR Review Reports issued
Close-Out	• Project Sponsor (OR Manager) to close out OR Activities as per Project Close-Out by Project Manager • Project Manager to align and reflect outcomes of OR Close-Out into overall Project Close-Out	• OR Trials successfully conducted • OR Close-Out Report issued
PIR	Project Sponsor (assisted by OR Manager and/or Project Governance Manager) to review the effectiveness of OR Outcomes (e.g., "actuals" as compared to "planned" results)	OR Effectiveness Report issued, as part of the PIR Report

on the basis that the "products of the project" will actually have a "willing" customer. The official signing thereof must have occurred before Construction starts.

However, the Solution-System will eventually be taken "out of service". "The lifecycle for any system-of-interest must encompass not only the Development, Production, and Utilisation Stages but also provide early focus on the Retirement Stage when decommissioning and disposal of the system will occur"[23] – which entails activities to dispose of the "old solution", except when such a "system" will be renovated, upgraded.

Slack also raises the issue of "end-of-life" responsibility: "Either through legislation or consumer pressure, businesses are having to invest in processes that recycle or reuse their products after disposal".[52] Similarly, at eventual system-disposal, Operational Readiness must be "reversed" to the extent that facilities and supply/support systems are safely removed and the "environment" returned to its original (or better) state[45] – for nuclear plants, mines, refineries, etc., turn into hazardous liabilities if left in dereliction.

Therefore, "Deactivation and disposal considerations should be a part of the concept selection criteria",[19] says Forsberg. Further, INCOSE states,

> Planning for disposal is part of the system definition during the Concept Stage ... Early in the 21st century, many countries have changed their laws to hold the creator of a system-of-interest accountable for proper end-of-life disposal of the system.[23]

Disposal is planned in!

As a result, system designers might be faced with complex trade-offs,[32] although it is not always easy to secure all the information that is needed to make the "best" choices. "For example ... using strong material, over-designed components, ample corrosion protection, and so on. But its production might use more materials and energy and it could create more waste on disposal. To help make more rational decisions in the design activity, some industries are experimenting with life cycle analysis [or LCA]".[52] This "life cycle analysis" is a technique that analyses all the production inputs, lifecycle use of a product and its final disposal in terms of total energy used and wastes emitted. LCA promotes a smooth, waste-less "reversal" of Operational Readiness at Disposal.[52]

Furthermore, while it is indeed imperative to achieve Operational Readiness at Ramp-Up (when transitioning from the project realm to operations), maintaining such a level of readiness throughout operational stages is also critical. Therefore, upon attaining Operational Readiness, a viable Continuity of Operations Plan (COOP) is needed that details how essential functions of Systems Operations should/will be sustained during emergencies or disruptions to normal operations (e.g., when systems or facilities are damaged and/or inaccessible). For similar reasons, "brown-field" projects should also consider devising a "Back-Out" Plan. The "system" must be able to safely resume its operations, should transitioning to "future state" turn out unsuccessful or undesirable.

It is common cause that the *Titanic*[4] was the largest and most complex ship afloat at that time, and was thought unsinkable. But disaster struck during its maiden voyage on 14 April 1912, resulting in the reported deaths of 1,503 people (among them 885 crew and a seven-man band, who last sang "Nearer my God to Thee"). It carried 20 lifeboats, although 64 would have been required to rescue all on board. It is therefore safe to say that the "Unsinkable *Titanic*" had inadequate "readiness for emergencies".

The large-scale infrastructure environment has changed drastically in recent years, with tsunamis, pollution-causing disasters, and new threats such as weapons of mass destruction, terrorist attacks, and technological emergencies.

This ever-changing threat environment requires a Continuity of Operations Plan with the capability of enabling Business Continuity (i.e., systems to continue essential functions across a variety of emergencies, including "instability caused by war and/or terrorism or natural disaster and disease"[52]).

The objective of a COOP is "To help operations avoid and recover from disasters while keeping the business going".[52] This might be achieved through the following:

(1) By protecting essential facilities, equipment, tie-ins, records, and other assets;
(2) By ensuring the continuous, unimpaired performance of a system's essential critical functions and operations;
(3) By reducing or mitigating disruptions to operations – by identifying and assessing emergency risks;
(4) By reducing loss of life and minimising damages and losses to environment; and
(5) By achieving a timely and orderly recovery from an emergency and resumption of full service to customers – e.g., large-scale operations may expect recovery of critical functions within 12 hours by using "replacement offices".

Therefore, the COOP regimen shall maintain a permanent "activated" status. For instance, Kossiakoff advocates

> Systems that do not operate continuously but that must be ready at all times to perform when called upon [e.g., power generators, overflow valves, escape hatches] are usually subjected to periodic checks during their standby periods to ensure that they will operate at their full capability when required.[32]

Lack of regular maintenance and/or dry-runs of drills can prove fatal when disaster eventually strikes. The Bhopal Plant Disaster (India) occurred on the night of 2 December 1984, killing more than 200 people.

> The refrigeration system designed to keep MIC [or Methylisocyanate] storage tanks cool, had been turned off several months before and the freon drawn off for use elsewhere … The firewater spraying

systems designed to deal with fires, cool down overheated equipment, or provide supplementary water neutralization of gasses was operational but the spray could not reach the top of the flare stack.[47]

Had the refrigeration and fire water spraying "systems" been maintained and ready to perform in any emergency event, fewer people would have died that night. It would appear that negligence occurred. The human factor (e.g., incompetence, negligence, oversight, error, misuse) does play a key part in causing failure across many industries.

7 Focus on Human Capital Readiness

Human Capital Readiness is the most complex and onerous of OR Parameters due to the dynamic nature of human elements, "especially in the operations function, where most 'human resources' are to be found".[52] People will often react to and, contrariwise, affect changes, even as operability failure can arise from human factors.

For example, FoxMeyer Drugs was the fourth largest distributor of pharmaceuticals in the US, worth $5 billion in 1993. In a bid to increase efficiency, FoxMeyer purchased an SAP (software) system and a warehouse automation system, then hired Andersen Consulting to integrate and implement the two "strategic initiatives" in a US$ 35 million project. System Deployment, regrettably, proved disastrous due to adverse human factors.[57]

FoxMeyer warehouse employees whose jobs were affected (i.e., threatened) by the automated system were unsupportive of the project. After three existing warehouses were closed, the first warehouse to be automated was plagued by sabotage, with inventory damaged by workers, orders going unfilled, etc. By 1996, the company was bankrupt. FoxMeyer was eventually sold to a competitor for a mere US$ 80 million[57] – just 1.6% of its initial market capitalisation; a single project had sunk the company.

Worse still, "the new system turned out to be less capable than the one it replaced ... FoxMeyer sued Andersen and SAP for $500 million each, claiming it had paid twice the estimate to get the system in a quarter of the intended sites".[57] Of course, "ERP implementation is expensive ... partly because of the need to customize the system, understand its implications on the organization, and train staff to use it".[52]

The FoxMeyer saga is no isolated incident. According to GP Strategies (a global company based in the USA), Human Capital Readiness failures have caused delays in 73% of projects and budget overruns in 64% of projects in the Oil and Gas sector.[22] Such failures manifest themselves as

Start-Up delays, operational errors, occupational injuries, staff shortages, labour strikes, quality losses, or cost increases; in short, slow or erratic Ramp-Up, which is bad for business.[12,51]

This shows how all elements of the "system" are affected by human performance.[53] "A company's workforce has become increasingly important to business success".[52] For it is people who get things done! In fact, even "economists indicate that human and information capital have become the critical sources of economic growth".[6] Operational Readiness therefore relies heavily on achieving Human Capital Readiness.

As stated earlier, the second and equally important goal of capital projects consists of reaching a State of Operational Excellence as soon as possible after Start-Up.[22]

Hence, improvements to the operational environment should involve Lean Operations: "Lean Thinking is a holistic paradigm that focuses on delivering maximum value to the customer ... minimizing wasteful practices",[23] "with perfect quality and no waste".[52]

Slack argues that,

> While any operation's current performance may be far removed from such ideals, a fundamental lean belief is that it is possible to get closer to them over time. Without such beliefs to drive progress, lean proponents claim improvement is more likely to be transitory than continuous. This is why the concept of continuous improvement is such an important part of the lean philosophy. If its aims are set in terms of ideals which individual organizations may never fully achieve, then the emphasis must be on the way in which an organization [i.e., its operations] moves closer to the ideal state. The Japanese word for continuous improvement is Kaizen, and it is a key part of the lean philosophy ... Arguably the most significant part of the lean philosophy is its focus on the elimination of all forms of waste.[52]

"Lean Thinking is the dynamic, knowledge-driven, and customer-focused process through which all people in a defined enterprise continuously eliminate waste with the goal of creating value"[23] – the removal of activities and behaviours that do not add value.

The first and most obvious type of waste is "Muda". This is any physical activity that does not add value. There are many categories of Muda: (1) Transport, (2) Inventory, (3) Motion, (4) Waiting, (5) Over-processing, (6) Over-production, and (7) Defects. However a rather insidious form of Muda relates to (8) Skills of Personnel. It reflects the failure to utilise the (available) "skills and knowledge" of employees effectively.[15]

The second type of waste is "Mura", which largely manifests itself due to inconsistencies or unevenness in operations (e.g., demand is not smoothed out and/or unfair demand is placed on company processes and people). Tackling Mura involves human factors, such as openness and cooperation in the supply chain, being flexible with system design, and focusing on creating standard workflows for operators (i.e., personnel).[15]

The third type is "Muri" (i.e., overburden), which arises from failures in the system such as a lack of standard operating procedures,[45] inadequate training, incorrect tools, improper resource allocation (e.g., working on processes that one is not trained on, poor ergonomics, unclear instructions, fluctuating demand, lack of proper/prescribed maintenance, unreliable processes, poor or non-existent communication channels).[15] Overburdening of human resources will cause Muri in the operational environment (e.g., plants), and even across the organisation.

It follows from the above discourse that all three types of waste in operations (e.g., manufacturing, production) are closely connected to Human Resources Readiness[45] (e.g., skills, personnel utilisation) in the intended operational environment. Therefore, "Lean Thinking" principles must be considered as well in addressing human elements.

The human resources function recruits and develops the organisation's staff, as well as looking after their welfare: "The manner ... an organization's human resources are managed has a profound impact on the effectiveness of its operations function".[52]

In view of that, Human Capital Readiness will necessitate changes, adjustments and/or improvements to several organisational aspects within the environment of the owner-organisation (or the delivery agent, in rare cases) to accommodate the deployment (or the realisation) of new "systems". These adjustments could apply to:

(a) Strategic Business Plans and their supporting Performance Measurement System;

(b) Resource Envelope (from inferred to indicated to actual) to match the demand of "personnel ... to train, operate, maintain, and support the deployed system"[23] – and System Disposal Planning, exploring the "demobbing" of operational staffs;

(c) Operational environments in or around the organisation, e.g., business alignment, workplace ergonomics, social responsibility initiatives, agreements with unions;

(a) Organisational Design (i.e., management redesign, organograms, new positions), and legally accountable structures or appointments (i.e., new, or changes thereto);

(b) Change Management initiatives to maintain organisational alignment, including "changes" to the organisational culture to lessen resistance to OR Implementation.

The above aspects range from strategy to structure to culture.

> Clearly, these changes in strategy and structure create new requirements for staff. People and teams must be able to relate to diverse cultures and style ... In addition, new structures put demands on people and teams to manage multiple bosses, to communicate electronically with people all over the globe and to be flexible and adaptive.[6]

Accordingly, additional support and/or collaborative tools (e.g., ERP, PMIS, BIM) will be needed.

> New strategies, structures, and staffing requirements create the need for adequate systems to support them ... They cannot perform the tasks of a project [nor of the operations function], but they enhance and support the individuals working on a project [or operations] from disparate locations ... The new team technologies help virtual teams function, but a high performing team [e.g., operations staff] still requires strong team development skills to maximize the usefulness of the technology.[6]

While the said restructuring of the organisation to allow System Realisation and Deployment (and subsequent Operations, Maintenance, and Disposal) largely takes place within a reasonably brief period of time, changing human or job elements often prove a strenuous, onerous process "to be handled with care". According to GP Strategies,[22] such human and/or job elements will include the following:

(a) Job profiles (to reflect new positions, new work practices);

(b) Labour analytics (e.g., histogram and/or manpower forecasts);

(c) Defining skill competencies (i.e., technical and non-technical);

(d) Commissioning team(s) – whether in-house or contracted-in;

(e) Key "Ramp-Up" skills – as required for operational tasks ahead;

(f) Recruitment drive and/or training and capacitation programmes;

(g) Adjusted HR systems (e.g., procurement and contractor recruitment processes, payroll, remuneration adjustments, succession planning, time-and-attendance routines); and

(h)   Any other elements that may influence human performance, based on Maslow's Pyramid of Needs – e.g., satisfying the self-actualisation (e.g., religion), social, and security needs of operational personnel assigned to remote or foreign locations.

Accordingly,

> A resource is any input required by a project ... including people, assets, materials, funding and services ... Organizations tend to overestimate their capacity ... When you're setting about your planning activities, carry out assurance reviews and perhaps even maturity assessment ... in order to understand the true capacity of the organisation.[18]

Still, many project managers do not budget for most of the above.

The author was appointed to "gate-review" a cross-border rail-link project involving railway companies from two neighbouring countries, with one company acting as the lead. The "single" business case initially suggested that the lead company would fund the rail infrastructure on both sides of the border. However, the other company has objected at the FEL-3 (i.e., Feasibility Study) Gate Review that the business case was flawed. Indeed, it was established at the FEL-3 that the paired company would need to increase its staff complement from 800 to around 1,400 people. Moreover, the required costs (and time) were not budgeted for in the approved business case. This was of great concern to them since recruiting, training, mobilising, and supporting 75% additional staff (all of that, almost overnight) would render the project unachievable!

The threefold demands of Availability, Capacity and Attainability of Human Capital required to ensure success, it follows, are heavily reliant on securing the appropriate skills (i.e., at the right levels and in the right numbers) through an appropriate training and capacitation scheme. A GP Strategies documentation suggests that a roll-out of Human Capital Readiness in Gas and Petroleum megaprojects is likely to take 22 months.[22] Late start and/or finalisation of training interventions may delay System Deployment or cause operability failure thereafter.

In addition, when planning for Human Capital Readiness, project teams must factor in the "Learning Dip" (i.e., the initial drop in job performance with new tools that will eventually improve to desired levels) and beware of people's "tendencies to revert to old ways". A positive "energy for change" that "institutionalizes positive behavior"[45] must be created by mobilising people and teams behind values, strategy, and structure.

Bellingham[6] laments:

> Unfortunately, most skill profiling efforts do not take into account all the demands imposed by changes in shared values, strategy, structure, staffing and systems ... We have found there are three key success factors in changing corporate culture efforts: commitment, capacity, and culture [i.e., mindset]. For any changes to be successful, [project] leaders need to have a simultaneous focus on all three factors ... We often hear organizations talk about people [i.e., staff] as the most valuable and valued asset, but we rarely see [or hear about] a consistent set of actions and initiatives that support those statements. In most organizations, that phrase is simply an empty slogan that causes more cynicism than commitment.

Human Capital Readiness development is a great opportunity to rectify this mistake, and to harness "Lean Thinking" principles on soft, human factors[45] – just as they are on hard processes of production/ manufacturing.

8 Re-engineering business processes

A company may have the most committed workforce in the world, but "capacity" is still required in order to be successful. "Building capacity means developing the people ... [but also] processes and technologies to achieve customer growth".[6] In fact, the underlying logic behind the allocation of resources in order to develop financial and strategic performance is that such "improved" performance will be achieved by delivering value for the customer − and value delivery will be achieved through "process" delivery.[54]

A process is a continuous and regular succession of actions taking place or carried on in a definite manner and aimed at achieving some result. It can thus be viewed as the place where "added-value" is created, or, in other terms, every process generates value added.[55] Moreover, "Processes constitute a network where the activities of a certain process serve to add value to the inputs deriving from the previous process".[55]

Tonchia[55] cites ISO 9000 (clause 2.4) to define a "process" as a "set of interrelated or interacting activities which transforms inputs into outputs". He remarks that,

> In order to run effectively, a company must identify and manage different processes which are interrelated and interdependent. The output of a process is often an input to another one, thus the systematic identification and management of the processes ... and the interaction of these processes can be summarized in the expression "process approach". The aim is ... to promote process approach in the management of a company.[55]

Kalamo refers to operational management as the administration of business practices to create the highest level of efficiency possible (i.e., Operational Excellence) within an organisation.

It is concerned with converting inputs (Materials, Labour) into outputs (Services, Goods) as efficiently as possible to maximize the profit of an organization ... operational management involves overseeing, designing, controlling the process of production, as well as redesigning business operations.[29]

It is all about processes!

A "business process" consists of a set of activities. Each activity is formed by elementary operations, requires specific resources, and is aimed at a goal that concurs with those of all the other activities to achieve the objective of the process, an objective that integrates all the goals of the different activities.[55] However, "Traditionally, each function tries to maximise its result in relation to its goal-parameters, but this may be in contrast with the overall objectives of the enterprise".[55] Thus, attempts to effect "operational improvements" may worsen the situation, by magnifying a dysfunction. Indeed, effective and efficient business processes are required in order to successfully implement business strategies.[54] Hence, "Badly designed processes, inappropriate products, poor locations ... or forgetting the importance of continually improving quality, could all turn a previously successful organization into a failing one".[52] Issues such as these easily arise when an infrastructure project seeks to improve "operations".

Now, Slack offers a generic definition of "operations" that highlights business processes:

> Put simply, operations are processes that take in a set of input resources which are used to transform something, or are transformed themselves, into outputs of products and services ... all operations conform to this general input–transformation–output model, they differ in the nature of their specific inputs and outputs. For example, if you stand far enough away from a hospital or a car plant, they might look very similar, but move closer and clear differences do start to emerge. One is a manufacturing operation producing "products", and the other is a service operation producing "services" that change the physiological or psychological condition of patients.[52]

Further, the point was made earlier (in Chapter 2) that projects are primarily for the sake of "operations", in order to improve (or establish) the Operational Environment. Successful infrastructure delivery will necessitate "adjustments" to existing (or offer an opportunity to develop new) "business processes" to support Operational Excellence.

Such operational processes cut across various functional areas. "Working effectively with the other parts of the organization is one of the most important responsibilities of operations management. It is a fundamental [notion] of modern management that functional boundaries should not hinder efficient internal [business] processes".[52] The Porter's Value Chain Model[48] shows the way in which the various activities of an organisation work together to add value (Margin) in the eyes of the customer[52,55] (see Figure 8.1).

The ways these activities (of "operations", in particular) function and interrelate across the value chain constitute an organisation's processes. Thus, Bogdănoiu contends, "In cross-functional organizational units the main organizational unit is the process. Since 'doing business' is mainly running processes, it would be very logical to organize companies based on processes".[7] Ineffective processes will cause business failure. For example, informational asymmetries arising from the project, and their resultant problems of cooperation and coordination within the "expanded" organisation (due to its improved operations) may cause a business to fail altogether.[51] Process is the key!

Effective business processes are essential to an organisation's success in producing its goods and services. For an organisation to maximise its competitiveness it needs to have processes that are well designed and that work effectively. Process is key to organisational "metabolism".

> One will see that all operations consist of a collection of processes (though these processes may be called "units" or "departments") interconnecting with each other to form a network. Each process acts as a smaller version of the whole operation of which it forms a part, and transformed resources flow between them. In fact within any operation, the mechanisms that actually transform inputs into outputs are these processes.[52]

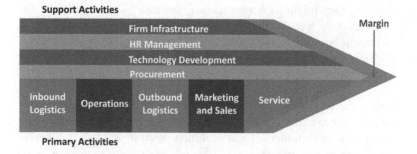

Figure 8.1 Porter's Value Chain Model, as per Porter[48]

Thus, completing an infrastructure without mending operational processes may prove futile.

Figure 8.2 illustrates somewhat dysfunctional business processes pertaining to a "lab & bulk chemicals" business. It emerges from the summarised processes that: (1) Finance may send invoices to customers for goods not received or even out of stock, (2) such invoices will not concur with receipt of goods, (3) goods could be dispatched for wrong invoices, and (4) Finance could be flooding warehouses with new stock, though actual transactions might not justify doing so. Building a "mega-warehouse" (i.e., infrastructure) without mending business processes will only worsen the predicament. Operational improvement may in fact be effected just by mending business processes.

Unfortunately, many infrastructure projects have been initiated against a background of perceived needs arising from deficient or dysfunctional processes; bigger structures were built for "perceived needs" that smarter processes could easily have addressed.

Indeed,

> The experience of the Municipal Corporation of Greater Mumbai provides an example of weak planning in the water sector. The Corporation was looking for ways to improve the efficiency of its operations. Mumbai is short of water, with supply rationed to around four to six hours a day in most parts of the city. Corporation planners were working on new schemes to transport water from hundreds of kilometres outside the city.[58]

This was per their usual stance until

> Consultants engaged through the World Bank analyzed the cost of achieving a 24-hour water supply in one ward (K-East) entirely with

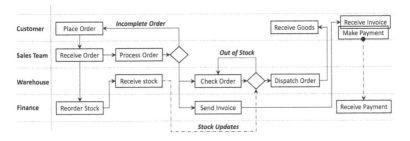

Figure 8.2 Example of order fulfilment process diagram

new supply, and compared this with the cost of achieving 24-hour water supply through improving the distribution system to reduce leakage and theft. The consultants estimated that the cost of distribution improvements would be one-sixth or less of the cost of bulk supply increments, for the same level of service improvements. The size of the discrepancy suggests that the Municipal Corporations' planning had been biased toward large projects.[58]

Similar patterns are also being observed in Southern Africa.[1] The author was once appointed to "gate-review" a port project at Pre-Feasibility stage. He insisted that "operations" teams be included in the process so as to understand the implications of the proposed options and ratify the rationale behind the choice of the "single-go-forward" option. It then emerged they had already identified "operational rearrangements" that could deliver more throughput, at a cost 40% of the estimated capital budget, and take only 6 months to execute. The capital project was not needed; continuing with the idea would have had adverse effects on the company's operations, not to mention the negative implications to its income statement and balance sheet!

The LIPs industry is replete with examples of capital projects that might never add value. A McKinsey report[58] on infrastructure investment – identifying $57 trillion globally required between 2013 and 2030 – notes that scaling-up best practice (i.e., holistic planning that considers rearrangements of operational processes, not just capital) could save an average of $1 trillion a year in infrastructure costs during that period.[58] The above figures alone should compel infrastructure planners to consider operational rearrangements (i.e., process improvements) before initiating infrastructure projects.

Process-oriented organisations will endeavour to break down the barriers of structural departments and try to avoid functional "silos" – i.e., each department concentrating only on optimising its own function, rather than understanding how it contributes to overall value creation in the organisation, as a "system" to be optimised globally.[6,45]

Most business processes can be deconstructed into several subprocesses that each have their own attributes and components, but ultimately all contribute to achieving the goal of the overall strategic process (e.g., improved performance). It is nonetheless important to remember that, at whatever level it is being considered, a business process begins with a customer's need and ends with that need being fulfilled.[51,53]

---

1   Many governments pursue and encourage aggressive infrastructure investments to stimulate their economy – and as an instrument for job creation and GDP growth.

Indeed,

> Process management can be considered by all means a powerful catalyst for programmes aimed at customer satisfaction. It has in fact been designed to overcome problems related to the rigid structure of function-based organisations, where the different units and departments often have discordant performance goals.[55]

Hence, transitioning any "system" into operations without aligning and/or enhancing business processes in the intended environment will jeopardise the value offered to customers. This point remains: "*Capabilities are exploited in order to achieve outcomes ... [one has] to make some [process] changes in 'business as usual' in order to enable outcomes*".[18]

For a "process change" to be efficient and effective, it is crucial that the level of process change is appropriate for the process under review.

> However, the level of process change required is also likely to reflect the process capability maturity of the business. If the business has mature process capabilities, "process improvement" [e.g., Kaizen] efforts will be more or less continuous, undertaken by managers and their process teams. If a business has a low degree of process maturity then a "process redesign" [or reengineering] effort might be required to establish the initial process capabilities.[29]

The "accelerated" change most capital projects entail calls for a "process redesign" too; and Business Process Reengineering (BPR) is acclaimed as a process management tool. Pioneered by Hammer and Champy, the BPR method is "A fundamental reconsideration and radical redesign of organizational processes, in order to achieve drastic [e.g., accelerated] improvement of current performance in cost, service and speed".[7,51]

Bogdănoiu (citing Handy, 1990) states that the theory of "discontinuous thinking" is central to the BPR process, instead of the continuous (incremental) thinking that is largely derived from scientific thinking.[7]

> Business Process Reengineering involves changes in structures and in processes within the business environment. The entire technological, human, and organizational dimensions [i.e., operations] may be changed in BPR. Information Technology plays a major role in Business Process Reengineering as it provides office automation, it allows the business to be conducted in different locations, provides flexibility in manufacturing, permits quicker delivery to customers

... supports rapid and paperless transactions [– bad idea if dealing with dysfunctional "process"].[7]

Business Process Reengineering means not only change – but dramatic change. What constitutes dramatic change [e.g., to "operations"] is the overhaul of organizational structures, management systems, employee [roles,] responsibilities and performance measurements, incentive systems, skills development, and the use of information technology.[11]

When BPR is compared with the Kaizen method, BPR is harder to implement, is technology-oriented, and enables "radical" change. However, the Kaizen method is easier to implement, is more people-oriented, and requires long-term discipline.[7]

The Kaizen method is a management concept for "incremental" change – Kaizen follows BPR efforts. "Kaizen is focused on making small improvements on a continuous basis ... Business Process Reengineering is a 'project' with a defined beginning and end, and Kaizen never ending",[7] notes Bogdănoiu. The key aspects of Kaizen are quality, effort, the involvement of all teams, a willingness to change, and communication.[6,7]

The promise of BPR is not empty. It can actually produce revolutionary improvements for business operations. Re-engineering can help an aggressive company to thrive, or transform an organisation on the verge of bankruptcy into an effective competitor.[11]

However, Covert (1996) [11] deplores that,

> Recent surveys estimate the percentage of BPR failures to be as high as 70%. Some organizations have put forth extensive BPR efforts only to achieve marginal, or even negligible, benefits. Others have succeeded only in destroying the morale and momentum built up over the lifetime of the organization. These failures indicate ... reengineering involves a great deal of risk.[11]

Even so, many organisations are still willing to take that risk because the rewards can be astounding. Many unsuccessful BPR attempts may be due to the confusion surrounding BPR, and how it should be performed – not being aware that changes must be made, not knowing which areas to change or how to change them.[11,51]

Tonchia offers an effective BPR approach;

> The goals of every function must integrate in a synergic manner ... to achieve the objective of customer satisfaction. The processes, by exploiting the resources of the company's functions, define,

co-ordinate and target the activities towards the satisfaction of the external customer.[55]

Referring to Figure 8.2, the "dispatch order" should have been linked to stock availability and invoicing; and "reorder stock" ought to follow "stock updates", which will reduce warehousing needs.

Indeed, one of the more radical prescriptions of Business Process Re-engineering is the idea that operations should be organised around the total process that adds value for customers, rather than the functions or activities that perform the various stages of the value-adding activity. Identified customer needs are entirely fulfilled by an "end-to-end" business process. In fact, business processes are designed specifically to do this; therefore, they will often cut across conventional organisational boundaries.[52]

There is however no "one-size-fits-all" approach to BPR. "Because organizations differ, the activities required to successfully perform a BPR may also differ",[11] Covert argues. Therefore, citing Hammer and Champy (1993), Tonchia[55] has considered it useful to identify precisely the "actors" in the process re-engineering exercise as follows:

- A leader (a high-level manager who authorises and endorses the BPR changes);
- A managerial committee (including top management and various area managers, and chaired by the "leader", who defines and develops re-engineering strategies);
- A process owner for each main process proposed (in charge of the selected process and its re-engineering);
- A re-engineering team (a group committed to the integrated re-engineering of the processes, with delegates from the various macro-processes identified);
- A person in charge of improvement and re-engineering (who must develop and implement it, by coordinating the different, related actions).

Citing the same source, Tonchia[55] recommends the following implementation steps:

(1) Begin Organisational Change – assess the current state, illustrate the desired state, and create a communications campaign for change;
(2) Build the Re-engineering Organisation – establish a BPR organisational structure, establish the roles for performing BPR, and choose the team who will re-engineer;

(3) Identify BPR Opportunities – identify the high-level processes, pri-
    oritise selected processes, determine customer's actual needs, and
    identify implementation risks;

(4) Understand the Existing Processes – understand the "why" of cur-
    rent steps, model the current process, understand how technology
    or information is currently used;

(5) Re-engineer the Processes – question operating assumptions, brain-
    storm using change levers and using BPR principles, evaluate the
    impact of new technologies, and use customer value as the focal point;

(6) Blueprint the New Business System – define the new flow of work,
    model the new process steps, model the new information require-
    ments, and document the new organisational structure and the new
    technology specifications.

(7) Perform the Transformation – develop a migration strategy, educate
    staff about the new process, and incorporate process improvement
    mechanisms.

One critical element of the above implementation steps (Step 6) entails
developing a "blueprint"[18] that details all the changes envisioned for the
process re-engineering. Moreover, Yetton and Craig (1994)[60] submit that,
"The innovation of BPR lies in rolling together, into one activity, the two
steps of conducting a strategic analysis (identifying core business processes)
and developing a detailed blueprint for the new vision (redesigning those
processes)". Further, devising a blueprint is crucial in guiding the re-engineering efforts (e.g., communicating with stakeholders, assessing progress).[18]

Shukla (citing Meyer and Attenborg, 2008) discusses the "Telenor and
Telia Merger":

> The two leading Scandinavian telecomm corporations decided to
> merge in year 1999 ... The Financial Times claimed that the merger
> would be a "Jewel of Communication" ... But soon afterwards the
> situation grew grim and the two companies decided to chuck off
> the deal. The major cause being incompatible corporate strategy,
> language and the governance structure ... Conflicts also emerged in
> the top management. There were also many differences in organiza-
> tional structure [and in the processes] too.[51]

This fiasco might not have occurred, had the merged companies agreed
to a "blueprint".

> In BPR, blueprints must be created to identify all the necessary
> details of the newly reengineered business system and ensure it will

be built as intended ... Blueprinting involves modelling the new process flow and the information required to support it ... The blueprints should also contain models of the redesigned organizational structure. Instead of the traditional organization chart, a different kind of chart is needed. This chart will show the new process flow along with the process team members, the process owners, the case managers, the process facilitators ... Included in the blueprints should be the new management systems and values or belief systems of this redesigned area of the business [i.e., in anticipation of Operational Excellence].[11]

Hereafter, project and change management tools shall assist in effecting the blueprint.

9 Operational Readiness Implementation

Operational Readiness (OR) essentially seeks to prepare the operational environment in order to receive the newly developed "system". As such, an Operational Readiness exercise should seek to satisfy five essential Operational Readiness and Operational Excellence considerations – i.e., safety, efficiency, effectiveness, reliability, trust.[22,51]

(1) Safety – i.e., freedom from those conditions that can cause death, occupational illness, injury, and damage to or loss of equipment or property, or damage to the environment;
(2) Efficiency – i.e., a measure of the extent a system is producing the maximum output from the input that goes into a process, or how well it is being used for the intended purpose;
(3) Effectiveness – i.e., a measure used to quantify the performance of a system, product, or process in terms that describe and/or measure to what degree real objectives and/or goals are achieved;
(4) Reliability – i.e., the probability that a device, product, or system will not fail for a given (i.e., continuous) period or under specified operating conditions; and
(5) Trust – i.e., relationship-building and trust between the relevant parties is a non-quantifiable quality that, while no substitute for good processes, makes human interactions agreeable. For instance, all the above-mentioned aspects increase trust in the workforce that Ramp-Up goals will be attained.

The above Operational Readiness and Operational Excellence considerations are to be addressed concomitantly in the "environment" through a robust OR Implementation. This, again, must shift the focus of project delivery from constructability to operability.

Moreover, any robust OR Implementation is likely to introduce the complex dynamics of homeostasis.[56] Assuming the operational environment and its adjacent broader environment are "in equilibrium" at the outset of a particular project, implementing Operational Readiness in that environment will entail over-riding the forces of homeostasis (i.e., the ability of the system to adjust its internal environment to maintain a state of dynamic equilibrium) before the desired changes or adjustments will take place. Indeed, Kasser has maintained[30] "From a homeostatic or self-regulating perspective the system strives to maintain a steady state of operational readiness".

It follows from this observation that a degree of homeosis (i.e., transformation of a system or structure from one status to another, *in an orderly mode*) is needed to effect a "conversion" of that environment from the "As Is" (status quo) to the "Should Be".[1] A *disorderly* transformation (e.g., against an entity DNA) will breed "hopeless monsters".

Bellingham upholds the need to manage any changes arising from OR Implementation:

> To the extent that you implement the action plans you have developed for your organizations, these changes will have significant implications for you and for the people in your organization ... Even positive events demand skills to manage change. In a simple sense, change means that things are not, and may never be, what they once were. Change involves a disruption of existing activities and feelings and requires learning new ways of doing things.[6]

Effecting change requires a "positive energy"!

Anyone who has worked in a difficult project would know the power for commitment: committed people bring a unique kind of energy to making projects successful.[43]

> Mobilizing people and [OR] teams behind the values, strategy and structure creates positive energy for change [herein referred to as "organisational energy"]. When there is a positive energy, people are able to produce more with less effort. When there is positive energy, people and teams use available technologies to communicate and participate. They are more focused on the possibilities and have an excitement about the renewal effort [OR Implementation, in this context]. Instead of wasting energy on complaints and negativity, there is an infectious vitality that enables people to focus on achieving business results.[6]

If still in doubt, go and ask Sisyphus (i.e., Greek legend).

It follows that a certain amount of "organisational energy" will be exerted to overcome "homeostatic equilibrium" (and related entropy) and then, through homeosis (i.e., well-orchestrated transmutation of a system), to transform the operational environment from the "As Is" to a "Should Be" state that accommodates the system to be deployed.

Kasser gives the perfect example to illustrate this point:

> If the system (molecules of water) begins at a temperature below zero degrees centigrade and is heated [i.e., by exerting energy], the behaviour of the ice is homeostatic until the melting point of ice is reached and the system goes through a transition phase changing state to water. As the liquid is heated further, the water then exhibits homeostatic behaviour until the temperature reaches the boiling point and a further state change to steam takes place.[30]

In the example, heat energy is used to defeat equilibrium and effect change.

The said homeotic transformation of the operational environment may only take place within the confines of the "carrying capacity" of that Systems-of-Interest, including the Realisation-System, the Solution-System itself, and the Context-System. The "carrying capacity" of any such "environment" derives from its total capacity to provide resources to and absorb (dis-)benefits caused by change initiatives being effected.[39] Meadows thus argues

> any change that overtakes the "carrying capacity" of its "environment" will overshoot and collapse ... and in the process decrease the ultimate carrying capacity by consuming some necessary nonrenewable resource ... collapse occurs because of nonrenewable resource [e.g., raw materials, tolerance for change] depletion.[39,38]

While "organisational energy" could be boosted (through hiring, training, motivating), "natural endowments" (e.g., minerals, fossil fuels, freshwater, arable land) are limited. An assessment is needed before launching new projects as to their impacts on the available "carrying capacity". Again, many project sponsors have learned this the hard way. It is not automatic that electricity, water, and land are available for more projects.

The question of what pertinent organisational levels should undergo this homeotic transformation may also arise. The Viable System Model (VSM) affords an answer.

> VSM offers a way of gaining both functional decentralisation and cohesion of the whole. It is underpinned by fundamental cybernetic principles of communication and control in complex organizations.

These [systemic] principles offer a way of providing true autonomy and empowerment within an integrated framework, together with the necessary supporting links between the individual parts. In short, the VSM provides a [basic, yet effective] framework for designing flexible, adaptable organizations that balance external and internal perspectives and long and short-term thinking.[16,17]

The Viable System Model was created by Stafford Beer over 20 years ago and has been used extensively as a conceptual tool for understanding organisations, redesigning them (where appropriate – e.g., as part of OR Implementation in complex and large-scale projects) and supporting the management of change.[16,17]

In line with the homeotic transformation,

Organisation redesign efforts [arising from Operational Readiness, for instance] and communication/information infrastructures can be directed towards achieving viability for the organization at [the] least cost – financially, materially and in people terms ... An autonomous unit (or viable system) [at any level of the owner-organisation] needs to have five key systems in place if it is to operate effectively in its [holistic] environment. These are Implementation [i.e., the core of Operations, dotted-circle], Co-ordination, Control, Intelligence and Policy[16] (see Figure 9.1).

(1) Implementation – Primary activities are responsible for producing products or services as per the organisation's identity and are core to the recursive model;

(2) Coordination – Any viable system has systems in place to coordinate the interfaces of value-adding functions and the operations (i.e., Implementation) of its primary subunits. Coordination is the element that "dampens" the volatility (or oscillations) caused by conflict between parts of Implementation;

(3) Control – A two-way communication between subunit and meta-level unit remains a prerequisite for viability (i.e., channel for instructions, reporting, and resources negotiations). It shall guide the organisation towards its objectives;

(4) Intelligence – A two-way linkage between the primary activity and its external environment is fundamental to adaptivity, for providing primary activity with continuous feedback on marketplace conditions, future trends, etc.;

(5) Policy – The policy-making function is the thinking part of the organisation and is responsible for the direction of the whole organisation.

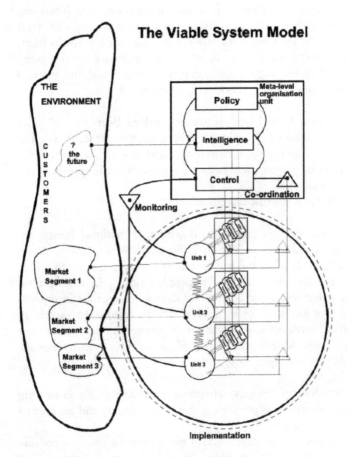

Figure 9.1 Viable System Model, adapted from Espejo[16]

> By definition, it is of low variety (compared to the previous items) and needs to be highly selective in information it receives through its continued interactions with Intelligence and Control functions, thus arbitrating between these two key systems.[16,17]

Alongside viability, the concept of "recursivity" considers the architecture of complex organisations. Since all "living systems" are composed of a series of subsystems, each ought to have self-organising and self-regulatory characteristics. From this principle, it follows that "expanding" the Implementation domain will entail adjustments (in both structure and capacity) to the Coordination, Control, Intelligence, and Policy "systems" of that organisation. For example, a car maker that expands by acquiring a tyre factory ought to correspondingly "expand" in their supply chain, costs budgeting/reporting, R&D/marketing, and business planning. Anything less will threaten business viability. These adjustments could affect the legal and statutory, human resources, operational processes, utilities/infrastructure, and commercial aspects of the "aggregated" entities.

Sadly, scores of infrastructure projects have failed to reach design capacity owing to "organisational adjustments" being ignored at some higher "systems" of its operational environment. One could think of road/railway network projects that might have been satisfactorily delivered at operational level (thus, increased road/rail transit capacity), but that still failed to provide the transportation benefits to a particular region due to a dysfunctional "Coordination System" (e.g., lack of connecting buses) or to an unsuitable "Intelligence System" (e.g., tariffs raised far above commuter affordability).

The use of the VSM as an OR Implementation framework will avert such predicaments.

In "A Case Study Evaluation of the Use of the Viable System Model in Information Systems Development", Kawalek and Wastell (1999) maintain:

> This paper considers the usefulness of the Viable System Model (VSM) in information systems (IS) projects. The VSM is a rigorous organizational model ... The paper presents a case study that focuses upon the sales team of a manufacturing company. This sales team were seeking to develop a database support for group working. The VSM was useful in highlighting the organizational limitations upon the IS project and challenged some assumptions about the nature of work in the company. It is proposed that the VSM provides a valuable diagnostic capability [e.g., for redesign, as needed] that shall assist the company in future IS developments.[31]

Hence, the VSM, as a tool, shall assist any organisations in implementing Operational Readiness (as a homeotic transformation).

Successful OR Implementation requires a VSM-based OR Blueprint[1] and a robust OR Plan that details and addresses most delivery parameters (e.g., objectives, scope, resources and structures, costs, timelines, and major risks) pertaining to the planned OR Implementation. Such an OR

---

1 OR Blueprint is a coherent "Should Be" state, reflecting to what specific VSM-state the OR Scope, once fully implemented, is expected to ultimately transform the "As Is" state.

Plan is best executed by the appointed OR and/or Change Manager. The scope, costs, timelines, and risks of OR Implementation shall also feature in both Project Execution Plan (PEP) and Business Case (BC) documents.

As an experienced Delivery Director, Helfrich has argued that "You can avoid the delays experienced by Terminal 5 and build confidence in your new system by, [i]fully testing business processes, [ii]giving users early access, and [iii]establishing critical, go-live communication protocols". She submits that these three Operational Readiness steps, among others, are essential to the success of complex, large-scale projects.[24]

From this expert advice, it is clear that OR Implementation should be project managed. Thus, once the "Scope" of Operational Readiness is established, a structured Project Management approach is needed to satisfactorily carry out the required OR activities. Good practice will suggest treating OR activities like any other "core" project activities (see Table 9.1).

OR Implementation should incorporate four essential components as summarised in Figure 9.2. Moreover, both OR Blueprints and Plans

Table 9.1 Key components of Operational Readiness Plan

Operational Readiness (OR) Plan		
OR aspect	Description	Artefacts
OR Objectives	What safety, efficiency, effectiveness, reliability, and trust targets will best contribute to attaining Operational Readiness objectives?	OR Hierarchy of Objectives
OR Scope	What elements of legal, human capital, processes, infrastructure, and commercial domains are needed to attain the agreed OR objectives?	OR Activity List, WBS
OR Resources	Human Resources (i.e., skills, capacity, teams, structures) that are required to carry out the OR Plan and to sustain ensuing Operations	OR Org Chart, Histograms
OR Costs	Capex and Opex arising from OR Implementation (i.e., effect changes and adjustments to the Context-System), as a result of the project	OR Budget, Cash-flow
OR Schedule	Timelines and Dependencies to consider in terms of activities arising from the execution of the OR Scope, leading up to subsequent PIRs	OR Milestones, Gantt Chart
OR Risks	Key risks (i.e., threats and opportunities) to consider and address in terms of activities arising from the execution of the OR Scope	OR Risk Plan, Risk Register

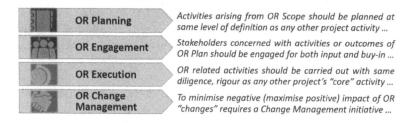

OR Planning	*Activities arising from OR Scope should be planned at same level of definition as any other project activity ...*
OR Engagement	*Stakeholders concerned with activities or outcomes of OR Plan should be engaged for both input and buy-in ...*
OR Execution	*OR related activities should be carried out with same diligence, rigour as any other project's "core" activity ...*
OR Change Management	*To minimise negative (maximise positive) impact of OR "changes" requires a Change Management initiative ...*

Figure 9.2 Components of Operational Readiness Implementation

(at project level) should be integrated at the programme and portfolio levels to achieve an effective and well-orchestrated OR Implementation across the whole organisation. OR Implementation should be effected as a "well-orchestrated trans-mutation" of the Context-System.[1]

The OR Scope should in fact be executed with the same rigour as the project scope. However, making it the responsibility of the project manager is generally problematic, as generally they are not in charge of the operational phase,[27] and thus have no jurisdiction or leverage over the Context-System. For this reason, it is advisable to appoint an OR Manager or a Change Manager for Operational Readiness roles; leaving OR Implementation to the project manager has often proved overwhelming.

Considering the core capabilities of most design partners (e.g., EPC/M providers) generally reside in designing and building systems, they exhibit a reduced focus on the operational support functionality. A suitably qualified, dedicated person, preferably from within the business/operational environment (e.g., OR Manager, Change and/or Benefits Manager), ought to execute the OR Plan[2], reporting to the Project Sponsor.[27]

> His/her roles should largely consist of ensuring that all the appropriate business and/or organisational systems and procedures and information requirements are in place, right from Operational Start-Up,

---

2 As a matter of fact,

> Benefits realisation [which relies on Operational Readiness] is the responsibility of the customer's organizational management, that may use the deliverables of the project to realise benefits in alignment with the organizational strategy. The project manager should consider the benefits and their realisation in so far as they influence decision-making throughout the project life cycle.

and effectively "operated" by competent personnel working together in a collaborative environment that is both safe and stable. For "trust is at the heart of collaboration ... people need one another in order to get things done. Commitment and collaboration are crucial in ... expediting matters", says Msengana.[43]

Trust capital, however, can easily be eroded during a misdirected OR Implementation. Also, most Team Effectiveness Models examine issues related to thrust (i.e., a common purpose about what needs to be accomplished or team goals), trust (i.e., in each of the team-mates), and learning skills (i.e., operating effectively as a team). Nevertheless, it is often the first two (thrust and trust) that will assure a successful OR Implementation. Various role-players need to appreciate and agree to the necessity and direction of the "orchestrated trans-mutation" so as to subscribe to it, accept the "burdens of change".

Regrettably, many managers in charge of OR Implementation are not likely to share any information with the rest of the organisation, fearing that they might not collaborate. This attitude is counterproductive: How does one expect internal teams to follow or actively participate in the homeosis of operations (which affect aspects of their jobs) without even understanding what might be going on? What the end-results might be?

The OR Manager, given the delicacy of human-related interventions, should thus exercise caution in executing capacity-building schemes as part of OR Implementation for "Attention to training, teamwork, and employee morale can help avoid risks".[23]

Whether teamwork was deemed effective or not before OR Implementation, there is still a need to address questions such as, "Is the team real rather than by name only?", "Does the team have a compelling direction?", "Is teamwork facilitated by an enabling structure?", and "Does the team operate within a supporting organisational context?". This approach to gauging team effectiveness lays a reliable canvas for improvements.

Due to their inherent complexity, human resources as a whole shall be appreciated as a Complex-Adaptive-System, capable of exhibiting undesirable "emergent" behaviours. Attempts by the OR Manager to impose a predetermined human capital regimen (e.g., skills, culture, structure) may yield undesirable results and prove counterproductive.

As far as personnel are concerned, raising the level of competence (e.g., qualifications, skills, experience) without concurrently improving their employment conditions (e.g., job content, salary) will lead not only to reduced job satisfaction (e.g., frustrations over work practices), but also set a noticeable upturn in marketability – many may soon leave! Such undesirable dynamics have the potential of collapsing Human Capital Readiness.

Hence, citing Land (2009), Jones suggests that

> Capacity building should not be carried out as part of a "deficit-based" or [rigid] blueprint-based approach. Rather, it should be approached in an "incremental" manner, combining a degree of formal strategic intent with a flexible design; taking an evolutionary approach to supporting programmes; working harder to ensure ownership is retained by responding to organisations' motivations, identities and needs; and being creative about options for support, embedded in the political, social and cultural norms within which they operate.[28]

This will call for a regular and timely review of the Human Capital Readiness in particular.

In fact, reviews of all readiness aspects will gauge the success of OR Implementation. ISO 21500 states, "The planning processes are employed for ... setting the baselines [i.e., success criteria] against which project implementation [i.e., OR Implementation] should proceed and project performance [in operations] should be measured".[27]

Furthermore, since Operational Readiness Requirements (together with the attributes of the Solution-System) govern the scope, timing, and technical and/or organisational parameters (e.g., success criteria, roles, and responsibilities) of Post-Implementation Reviews (PIRs), the appointed OR Manager shall, of necessity, initiate and conduct PIR sessions soon after Ramp-Up is complete and operations have somewhat stabilised.

10 Post-Implementation Review

Post-Implementation Review (PIR) is a crucial step in confirming that the "system as deployed" has effectively attained Operational Readiness (OR) and Operational Excellence and is delivering the expected benefits in line with the business case. For instance, how do the actual ROI and/or ROCE and other operational performance parameters compare against the projected ones?. It is sheer impudence to assume successful System Deployment and proceed to expect benefits realisation.

Accordingly, suitable mechanisms should be put in place to establish to what extent OR Implementation has allowed a safe and effective utilisation of the "system" in the intended operational environment. It is advisable that

> Once strategies have been implemented [through projects], the following step is to monitor and observe whether the intended improvement in system performance actually occurred. One should also be careful to identify ... unintended degradation in the performance of one subsystem [e.g., airport], due to policies aimed at another subsystem [e.g., bird population]. The capability to monitor the success of policy alternatives is often absent, and therefore one may include monitoring systems as part of the strategy for implementation.[14]

Therefore, Operational Readiness plays a vital role in securing an effective PIR; its timing should follow a successful Ramp-Up, after the system is notably stable, and is part of the day-to-day operations, which occurs some 6 to 36 months after handover.

In a railway project involving the manufacturing of specific coal wagons, the author observed that Post-Implementation Review requirements were clearly stated in the business case and were expected to run smoothly. However, as it turned out, the PIR Report proved inconclusive with respect to cost benefits, as there was no itemised cost-reporting mechanism in place. Even though the PIR Scope (i.e., what should be reviewed) was established, the team was not able to verify the "actual" maintenance costs of the newly built coal wagons. This inadequacy of the OR Scope (i.e., absence of measurement tools) rendered it difficult to verify the actual NPV against initial projections.

In addition, the PIR Report shall highlight flaws in the System Requirements as well as in its technical features. Interfaces between the system and its subsystems and their operational environment enable successful System Utilisation. Inconsistencies and/or deviations thereto might lead to corrective actions and requirement changes. Lastly, PIRs shall also reveal the gaps between the "real needs" and the "realised needs" of the owner-organisation, which are required for a successful OR Implementation. It might also prove useful conducting a PIR after system disposal to verify "site rehabilitation".

A consulting firm shared a peculiar PIR occurrence with the author.

> The Client needed an independent due diligence report [i.e., a form of PIR] on the design and construction of a major, new river crossing in Southern Africa in order to confirm compliance with original mandate before final project sign-off … A detailed due diligence report confirmed satisfactory completion, but identified some concerns with the original specification that had led to the bridge being over-engineered for the local conditions ([i]with consequent implications for the ability [or lack thereof] of the provincial infrastructure organisation to maintain the intricate bridge) and being supported with monitoring equipment that had been insufficiently protected ([ii]and was afterwards stolen).

Both issues evidently arose from Operational Readiness shortcomings.

For INCOSE[20] suggests that besides Verification and Validation (V&V)[1] activities, PIRs should include the following implementation aspects:

(a) Context-System dynamics and the negative impacts thereof (i.e., unanticipated changes to laws and policies, to socio-economic

---

1 The focus is placed on controlling the interfaces between system elements and external systems. It is especially important to ensure that the interfaces are still operational when an older component system is replaced with a newer version. Verification and validation (V&V) processes play a critical role in such transitions … Vee [Model] highlights the need to define verification plans during requirements development, the need for continuous validation with the stakeholders, and the importance of continuous risk and opportunity assessment.

drivers, and to operations and/or adjacent ecosystems might impose changes to the deployed system);

(b)   Delivery of business/operational benefits (or any contributions thereto) as per the business case – e.g., hierarchy of objectives, NPV or ROI/ROCE, operational benefits from a stakeholder's perspective;

(c)   Suitability of the Realisation-System (i.e., project requirements, planning and design assumptions, processes, tools and techniques, and skills utilisation) considering recorded "actual" operational performance;

(d)   Extent of attainment of Operational Readiness (and of Operational Excellence, post-Ramp-Up) – OR shall secure "operability", which PIR will verify and validate;

(e)   Analysis of any of the above considerations and other emergent issues to identify improvement areas;

(f)   Proposed Corrective Actions (in line with the organisational strategy); and

(g)   Lessons Learned, which shall apply to both the project realm and the business environments.

There is no need for an ongoing debate on whether PIR should be made a lifecycle-embedded, mandatory process. The author conducted a survey on Large Infrastructure Projects in Southern Africa (as of 2015[34]). It revealed that barely 32% of entities could boast of completing projects "*on time and on budget*". Despite this, 60% of entities did not consider PIR as a mandatory process, although 23% of participants could not tell whether "*Most projects meet their business objectives*", and still another 23% whether "*Most projects are completed to specifications*". These findings are quite remarkable!

Moreover, the same survey also revealed that only 41% of entities surveyed would agree that "*PIR is actually taking place*", while 18% could not even tell whether a "*PIR process/framework is in place*".[34] This "could not even tell" stance is worth noting!

The author submits that unless a robust OR Implementation is duly carried out, and PIRs are taking place at appropriate times (and preferably across the entire business or organisation, due to items (a), (b), and (e) above), either the deployed system will fail to reach Vertical Ramp-Up, or there will be no way of ascertaining that Operational Readiness was actually attained, and that a sustained Operational Excellence ensued. PIRs must also include the "broader" environment to assess possible damages thereto.

Unfortunately, the absence and inadequacies of Post-Implementation Reviews have deprived many industries of valuable lessons not only as to the root causes of operability failure, but also as to smarter ways and approaches to reaching Operational Readiness. They might fall in the trap of "drifting to low performance":[38] "Allowing performance standards to be influenced by past performance, especially if there is a negative bias in perceiving past performance, sets up a reinforcing feedback loop of eroding goals". Standards shall be influenced by the best actual performances, instead of by the worst.

11 Conclusion

Projects that deliver or upgrade systems should be completed on time, within budget, and to specification. This is the "triple-constraint" principle (a.k.a. iron triangle) of Project Management. However, many organisations have lost billions on projects that were satisfactorily delivered (i.e., passed commissioning with flying colours), but failed "to deliver value" in or to their operations. Of the many examples included in this book, the Heathrow Airport Terminal 5 and the New South China Mall are quite remarkable.

While both projects were satisfactorily completed and hailed as a feat of engineering and Project Management, Terminal 5 failed to operate effectively after inauguration due to shortcomings in the "system" itself (i.e., Transition Requirements not met). The colossal New South China Mall failed and was "abandoned" after opening due to the "environment" not being ready (or willing) to utilise it. Systems were satisfactorily completed, but benefits were jeopardised (Terminal 5), not realised (New China Mall).

Many other organisations involved in capital projects at some point wonder why they could not seem to get any real "bang" for all the "bucks" invested thus far for … well, something was not "ready" in their operations. Project Management should seek to go beyond the delivery of the physical infrastructure to pursuing the deployment (after such delivery) of a working "system" that provides improvements to the intended environment.

Unsurprisingly, a notable NETLIPSE (Network for the Dissemination of Knowledge on the Management and Organisation of Large Infrastructure Projects in Europe) finding was that

> Large Infrastructure Projects (LIPs) must be conceived, managed and operated as an integrated whole, focussing not only on the

completion of a physical project as an end in itself, but also on stakeholders involved ... LIPs are an important link for European transport [and for Africa] and on a higher level contribute to economic
and social sustainable growth of our society.[44]

According to ISO/DIS 21500 – Guidance on Project Management, it is
made plain that,

> A project usually exists within a larger organization encompassing
> other endeavours. In such cases there are relationships between the
> project and its [broader] environment, business planning and oper-
> ations. Pre- and post-project activities may include activities such
> as preparing the business case, conducting feasibility studies and
> transition to operations. Projects may be organised within other
> related structures such as programmes and project portfolios.[27]

So "transition to operations" is crucial!

Most statistics on project failure (e.g., Chaos Report, Prosperus
Report) suggest that a mere 32% of projects are "completed on time, on
budget and with required features functions"; 44% are challenged (e.g.,
late, over budget, and with fewer required features and/or functions),
and, sadly, as many as 25% are generally deemed outright failures.

It would therefore be sad, again, that a substantial portion of those
75% reasonably completed projects will subsequently fail to provide the
expected benefits owing to a poor/lack of Operational Readiness. But
the reality of the LIPs industry is not far from that!

According to GP Strategies, 64% of capital projects exceed their
original budget; as much as 30% of the original expected value can
be lost due to ineffective transition to operationalization; and 73% of
capital projects are delayed beyond their original scheduled launch.
Additionally, the Construction Industry Institute (CII) found that only
5.4% of 975 industrial projects met "best in class" predictability in terms
of cost and schedule. Definitely, such predicamental tendencies ought
to be reversed.

Project Management pursues a satisfactory completion of projects
(i.e., iron triangle); Operational Readiness (OR) supports project
delivery by ensuring that systems (i.e., products of projects) are "safely
received and effectively utilised" in their intended environment. In
turn, the operational environment should not impair the system either.
Operational Readiness plays a crucial role in delivering project benefits. Ideally, Operational Readiness should be implemented to ensure

a Vertical Ramp-Up, with near 90% of Design or Nameplate Capacity being attained at Start-Up.

The extent Operational Readiness is applied in an organisation correlates with project delivery maturity. The Portfolio, Programme and Project Management Maturity Model (P3M3®)[46] aptly reflects Operational Readiness as a key aspect of project delivery maturity as follows:

(i) Project management at Maturity Level 2: OR is reflected as a Management Control:

> concepts of project management will have been grasped by the organization, and there may be local experts, such as experienced project managers, working on key projects ... There will be active consideration of transition management [i.e., OR] to ensure that project deliverables are capable of being exploited by the user.[46]

Operational Readiness is expected as early as when reaching Level 2 "Maturity";

(ii) Programme management at Maturity Level 2: OR is to enhance Risk Management:

> Risk will be viewed in terms of aggregation and operational transition ... Risk management is recognized and used on programmes, but there are inconsistent approaches which result in different levels of commitment and effectiveness ... Some programmes recognize different categories of risk (e.g., by distinguishing between project and transition/operational risks);[46]

and

(iii) Portfolio management at Maturity Level 3: OR is to support Benefits Management:

> Business and service areas actively engaged in defining and realizing benefits ... Benefits realization objectives linked to operational business plans [subject to OR].[46]

The foregoing insights make it clear that Operational Readiness significantly enhances the probabilities of project success by preparing the end-user environment, not as an afterthought, but as an integral part of project delivery. In fact, the concept of readiness embraces five of the ten Project Management Body of Knowledge (PMBoK)[49] Guide's

Knowledge Areas, i.e., Scope, Time, Cost, Quality, and Risk – having a "system" more ready than its environment may prove fatal.

A recent Deloitte & Touche publication[12] boldly put forward that,

> It is increasingly recognised that a [deliberate] focus on operational readiness is a key differentiator in a programme's ability to deliver against the commitments in its business case. Programmes that embed operational readiness from the outset typically identify risks earlier, mitigate design issues when they are less costly to resolve and build highly capable teams ... Evidence suggests ... ongoing operations and maintenance costs over an asset's lifecycle are typically 1–2% higher, year-on-year and for the entire life of the asset, where operational readiness was not sufficiently achieved at the outset.[12]

The four Organisational Domains that must be addressed through OR are (1) Legal and Statutory, (2) Human Resources, (3) Processes, and (4) Utilities and Infrastructure. Commercial considerations such as the "readiness of customers" to procure and/or utilise the deployed system cannot be ignored. An enquiry on the Terminal 5 debacle pointed to items (2) and (3), whereas difficult access, which falls under item (4), and commercial issues (i.e., lack of customers) probably caused the New South China Mall to fail (due to poor or low occupancy). It is a costly mistake not to consider operability.

Decisive OR requirements will derive largely from two sources, namely: (1) Operational Requirements that drive changes to current or planned operations, and (2) Transition Requirements that support System Deployment during Transition, bridging into the "sustained" Operations. Both requirements must consider and address long-term sustainability of the system and, more importantly, that of the broader environment.

Common wisdom even reminds us that, "Neither do people pour new wine into old wineskins. If they do, the skins will burst; the wine will run out and the wineskins will be ruined. No, they pour new wine into new wineskins, and both are preserved" (Matthew 9:17). Putting new wine (i.e., a newly created "system") into an old wineskin (i.e., an unready operational/broader environment) would only be asking for it to "burst"!

Human Capital Readiness, in particular, will entail adjustments and improvements to a number of organisational aspects within the environment of the owner (or even the delivery agent, in rare cases) to accommodate the deployment (or even realisation) of the new Systems (e.g., product/output of projects). Not surprisingly, Human Capital Readiness is the most complex and onerous of OR parameters due to the dynamic nature of human elements. People react to and affect changes! Any OR changes shall, however, apply to all relevant organisational aspects of the operational environment. Thus, the accelerated change capital projects entail calls for a "process reengineering".

OR Planning and Implementation ought to evolve over the Project Lifecycle and include a Continuity of Operations Plan (COOP) that takes care of emergencies. A suitable OR and/or Change Manager should execute the OR Plan, including Post-Implementation Reviews (PIRs) and Disposal. This will ensure that activities (and impacts) flowing from the OR Scope are treated with the same diligence as any other "core" project activities. No "system" is deemed successful until it is successfully deployed in its operational environment. Successful commissioning and inauguration are only steps towards such.

While Heathrow Terminal 2 successfully transitioned into operations from day one, it must be noted that if the appointed Operational Readiness consultant had been involved from the project outset, the same (if not better) levels of readiness would have been achieved (on the opening day), but using far fewer organisational resources.

Recent studies have indicated that, (1) Retrofitting Operational Readiness (or applying it "at the tail end" of projects) may cost an additional 25% of Estimated Total Costs, and (2) Failure or lack of Operational Readiness may cause 30% loss of returns due to ailing or delayed Ramp-Up. This has the potential to defeat the viability of the business case, considering a cost overrun of 25% is sufficient to cause a project to fail altogether.[41] Operational Readiness, thus, requires adequate planning and robust implementation. Many LIP-delivery entities have overlooked Operational Readiness at their own peril.

12 Practical Operational Readiness applications

Readers who do not wish to "practice" Operational Readiness may skip this section.

The Project Management Body of Knowledge (PMBoK) 5th edition states, "Project Management is the application of knowledge, skills, tools, and techniques to project activities in order to meet project requirements".[49] Project Management is a practical discipline, whereby knowledge and skills, and tools and techniques, are applied in the pursuit of project success.

This chapter features four concise case studies that afford the reader an opportunity to begin putting into practice the concepts, principles, and practices discussed herein, even before challenges in their own project would require them to do so.

In addition to case studies, a recent article by the author and a paper by Moriarty and Honnery[42] discuss issues of operations and sustainability, reflecting that projects are primarily about improving (or establishing) the operational environment. Projects should therefore be initiated with the goal of making improvements to operations in mind. This is a fundamental Systems Engineering (SE) principle.[50]

It is hoped that through these practical examples, the reader may indeed grasp the intricacies of Operational Readiness (OR), upon which successful System Deployment depends. It is also hoped that, through the insights provided, the reader will be capacitated and equipped to make the connection between project and operational requirements.

There is no such a thing as "partially attained" Operational Readiness. One "missing" readiness-item could cause the operability of the whole "system" to collapse. Many developing countries are indeed finding themselves with largely "inoperable" military hardware (e.g., fighter jets, submarines, tanks) soon after their purchase, due to poor maintenance, lack of spare parts, or operators (e.g., pilots) having lost combat-fitness.

In another example, the introduction of electric locomotives was hailed as a "green" achievement by reducing diesel consumption. However, an upsurge in the mining and transportation of coal (which is "dirtier" than diesel) resulted in supply power plants needing to generate more electricity. The "burden" of the carbon footprint was not reduced, but shifted to another sector[38] in the same economy. Operational Readiness is never about the proverbial "robbing Peter to bless Paul", but rather about finding ways and means of blessing them both, as it were. This is no easy task, one will argue.

The journey to OR mastery might be long and taxing – yet practice shall make perfect!

12.1 Large Infrastructure Projects – Putting empathy in Operations [by the author]

How shall project teams apply their "hearts and minds" throughout the project lifecycle to ensure successful delivery?

We are still coming out of an era where the project manager's job revolved around either spending the budget or building the *damn thing*, namely completion of the physical deliverable(s) at any cost. Very few project practitioners appreciate that projects are *primarily* about improving (or establishing) the workings of the operational environment. It is our contention that no project should see the light of day *unless* it will add value to operations!

It is said, "Charity begins at home". Good projects begin with a deep appreciation of the operational needs. A good marriage does not start at the wedding but prior to it, from a shared perception of the kind of family the husband and wife intend raising. *Only upon such shall thy wed be locked*, or else divorce will soon loom (i.e., project failure).

Project teams often wallow through the mud of scope creep, cost and schedule overruns, and organisational politics with the hope that in the end "something new and great" will be standing where there was none before. Any concerns as to whether *that something* will add value by improving the operational environment (e.g., increased production, lower operating costs, improved quality of services, enhanced welfare) seem relegated to a bottom drawer – the one some reviewers might look into long after the project team has moved on to the next job.

When it comes to project delivery, and indeed in anything else in life, our charity should start at (the project's) home, at the operational environment where the delivered solution (e.g., new infrastructure, facility, and equipment) will be deployed.

Before a new project is launched, some stage of empathy is required. This should take place in the operational environment to gain a deep appreciation of ills, issues, challenges, and needs begging to be addressed in a technically and socio-economically viable manner. Only thereafter shall a project team revert to the conceptual phase and kick-start the project.

To return to our earlier analogy, locking the project's wed (i.e., launching the project) upon a lack of common understanding of project objectives, an evasive sense of agreement as to its worth, and a poor commitment to make it work is the harbinger of divorce or, in the project context, of project failure.

The question is: How will this "empathy" practically apply to your project? We maintain that a good project should start with an appreciation of operational matters (i.e., with the team planting their hearts in operations' concerns) and only then revert to the onset of the lifecycle, at the Conceptual phase or FEL-1 (i.e., whence the project team will apply their minds in planning and executing *infrastructural* elements that are lacking in that particular operational environment). The whole idea is to start with the end (e.g., improved operations) in mind, which is a Systems Engineering principle.

During this "empathy" phase, the project team should attain: (1) a shared perception about the project objectives, (2) a broad sense of agreement that the project is worth doing, (3) an expressed commitment to make it happen, and (4) elucidate items reflecting the operational environment from the sponsor and operational staff, including:

(i) Competing systems – facilities, equipment, and processes vying for resources with the system once deployed;
(ii) Collaborative systems – facilities, equipment, and processes that will collaborate with the deployed system;
(iii) Sustaining systems – facilities, equipment, and processes to support the operations of the deployed system.

Failing to secure the above ingredients, the project team would face the predicament of "building a puzzle over an *ever-changing* canvas". Despite all their efforts and creativity, only one thing is guaranteed: even when the pieces fit together, they will still fail to match the canvas. In our context this is deliverables that fail to add value to operations.

If the project team does everything else right (which many project professionals are capable of achieving) they might still disappoint the client (e.g., owner, sponsor) by delivering assets, facilities, and systems that turn into white elephants. Such "investments" will drain resources (e.g., capital outlay, operating and maintenance budgets) *ad infinitum* without adding value by improving the operational environment.

GreenPoint stadium (Cape Town, South Africa) was completed on-time and on-budget for the 2010 Soccer World Cup. Nevertheless, it is common knowledge that the charming Xhosa Lady (i.e., referring to its outline) is not adding much value to the city – it is forever gulping resources *just to keep standing pretty*, with hardly any hope of a steady income. (Are you surprised? Well, not too far from there, no large aeroplanes can land at the R 4.5 billion Saint Helena Island airport due to wind shear.) A mere trip in thought to its operational environment might have led to a "concept" that connected the stadium to the city's touristic sites (thus, making it a tourist attraction as well) and even secured revenues from rugby, cycling, etc. – for instance, albeit incidentally, the Moses Mabhida stadium (Durban) connects to beaches and thus attracts tourists. As it is, the city might join the public chorus baying for flattening of GreenPoint to make way for low-cost housing.

Worse still, the Spanish-built *Afro 4000* locomotives that PRASA procured in 2012 sparked a vivid controversy when it turned out that their height was *out of clearance specifications* (i.e., too tall for South African railways) and, thus, were failing to operate in many sections of the Transnet-owned network – billions of Rands got thrown off the rails. Then, as in a twist of irony, the infamous locomotives were finally *dumped* under the Nelson Mandela Bridge in Braamfontein.

What more should be said? Infrastructure delivery will prove vain *unless* acquired capabilities are effectively exploited in *improved* operations to derive the benefits and add value to the business. He who has ears to hear, let him hear!

12.2 Sustainability article [excerpt only]

AIMS Energy, 6(2): 272–290.
DOI: 10.3934/energy.2018.2.272
Received: 31 January 2018
Accepted: 23 March 2018 Published: 4 April 2018
http://www.aimspress.com/journal/energy

Review

Energy policy and economics under climate change

Patrick Moriarty[1,*] and Damon Honnery[2]

[1] Department of Design, Monash University-Caulfield Campus, P.O. Box 197, Caulfield East, Victoria 3145, Australia

[2] Department of Mechanical and Aerospace Engineering, Monash University-Clayton Campus, Victoria, Australia

* **Correspondence:** Email: patrick.moriarty@monash.edu; Tel: +61399032584.

Abstract: Most anthropogenic greenhouse gas emissions are the result of the combustion of fossil fuels. Proposals for mitigating climate change thus include various carbon dioxide removal technologies, replacement of fossil fuels by non-carbon alternatives (renewable and nuclear energy), and reduction in energy use overall by improving energy efficiency. We argue here that deep controversy surrounds the efficacy and likely costs of all these technical fix proposals. Optimistic conclusions are often drawn for these technical solutions partly because many of the analyses do not follow an Earth Systems Science approach. Instead, we argue that in future solutions based on nontechnical solutions will need to be a key approach for mitigating climate change in the short time frame we have left.

Keywords: carbon dioxide removal; climate mitigation; fossil fuels; energy costs; energy policy; energy return; Earth System Science; nuclear energy; precautionary principle; renewable energy; uncertainty

Abbreviations: BECCS: bioenergy carbon capture and sequestration; CCS: carbon capture and sequestration; CDR: Carbon dioxide removal; CO_2: carbon dioxide; CO_2-e: carbon dioxide equivalent; EJ: exajoule = 10^{18} joule; EROEI: energy return on energy invested; ESS: Earth System Science; GHG: greenhouse gas; GJ: gigajoule = 10^9 joule; Gt: gigatonne = 10^9 tonne; HANPP: human appropriation of Net Primary Production; IEA: International Energy Agency; IPCC: Intergovernmental Panel on Climate Change; LCA: Life Cycle Analysis; MJ: megajoule = 10^6 joule; NPP: Net Primary Production; OPEC: Organization of the Petroleum Exporting Countries; SCC: social cost of carbon

1. Introduction

The December 2015 Paris agreement committed the world's nations to limiting global temperature increases above the pre-industrial value to well below 2.0 °C, with an aspirational target of 1.5 °C increase. However, based on research reported in *New Scientist* [1], the world could breach the 1.5 °C limit as early as 2026. Anderson [2] has similarly argued that even 2 °C will be very difficult to achieve. But according to an analysis by climate scientists Xu and Ramanathan [3], any rise above 1.5 °C should be classed as "dangerous"—and increases above 3 °C as "catastrophic". A 2017 report [4] discussed the likely adverse consequences: for every 1.0 °C global temperature rise, wheat and rice yields are expected to decline by 6% and 10% respectively, and by 2050, a billion people, additional to the 125 million in 2016, will be exposed to deadly heat waves. Recent findings do not suggest that governments are taking climate change seriously, despite the rhetoric: according to Peters and his colleagues [5], annual carbon dioxide (CO_2) emissions from energy sources will rise by a projected 2% in 2017 to 37 gigatonnes (Gt), after no net growth from 2014 to 2016. Total CO_2 emissions, including net deforestation, are likely to be 41 Gt. The IEA, in their latest *World Energy Outlook* [6] have projected that global fossil fuel consumption will continue to grow until 2040, fuelled by population and economic growth.

Very clearly, we are entering uncharted and dangerous climate territory, and deep reductions in anthropogenic greenhouse gases (GHGs) are urgently needed. Since most of these emissions are related to fossil fuel energy production and combustion, the obvious question is: "What is the best way to greatly reduce energy GHGs, especially the dominant and long-lived one, CO_2?"

A key problem for energy policy is that the field of energy research relevant to climate change mitigation is beset by pervasive uncertainty. There are profound disagreements among reputable researchers on almost all topics of importance for making energy policy decisions. This disagreement is in marked contrast to the question of the reality of anthropogenic climate change itself, about which there is an overwhelming consensus among climate scientists [7]. An incomplete list of energy—related controversies would include the items presented in Table 1.

Table 1. Key energy controversies, and reference papers giving higher or lower values.

Energy controversy	Higher values	Lower values
Recoverable reserves for fossil fuels, especially oil	[8]	[9,10]
The technical potential for the various renewable energy (RE) sources	[8,11–14]	[15–24]
The Energy Return on Energy Invested (EROEI) and relative climate change benefits for the various RE sources	[25]	[26–30]
The time frames needed for these alternative fuels to replace fossil fuels	[31–35]	[36]
The likely monetary costs of these alternative fuels, compared with fossil fuels	[19,37]	[11,14]
Estimates of the social cost of carbon (SCC)	[38,39]	[40]
The technical potential for both biological CO_2 reductions and for various carbon capture and mechanical sequestration (CCS) methods, including from bioenergy (BECCS)	[41,42]	[43–46]
Costs for both biological CO_2 reductions and for various CCS methods, including BECCS	[47,48]	[41,42]

One way that can at least partly help resolve many of these controversies is to use an Earth System Science (ESS) approach [49]. In the context of climate change, this approach attempts to understand how all elements of the Earth system—atmosphere, biosphere, cryosphere, hydrosphere, biosphere, geosphere—interact to produce climate changes in the short- and long-term. More ambitiously, it also attempts to include human actions and responses into ESS modelling. In energy research and analysis, a parallel, if more restricted, approach is Life Cycle Analysis (LCA), which tries to document, for example, all the environmental and resource consequences of introducing a new energy technology compared with existing ones. Accordingly, this review mainly discusses papers with a global rather than a national or regional focus. Climate change is a global problem, and too often what looks like a solution at a national level merely displaces the problem elsewhere. As an example, the reduced energy-related CO_2 emissions in some OECD countries are largely the result of energy-intensive industry being shifted to Asia, particularly China.

This review is necessarily selective: entering in just the phrase "energy policy" into Google Scholar turned up nearly 800,000 hits. We thus focus on recent papers, since these in general will be based on the most up-to-date cost estimates, policy decisions (such as US withdrawal from the Paris climate agreement), and energy technology advances.

The rest of this review examines in turn the future prospects for each of the three competing energy sources: Fossil fuels, nuclear energy, and RE in its various forms. Each section examines the controversies given in Table 1, and attempts to reduce the areas of uncertainty. In the final, Discussion section, the implications of the preceding analysis are drawn out for energy policy, teasing out definite policy conclusions for global energy in a climate-constrained—and more generally, environment- and resource-constrained—world. Given that few of the controversies can be resolved with certainty, we urge an approach that is best able to deal with these. Accordingly, we advocate policies which rely less on technical fixes such as alternative fuels replacing fossil fuels and more on non-technical approaches based on re-examining the question of whether OECD countries in particular need to use so much energy at all.

2. Energy future: Fossil fuels

In attempting to forecast future energy, we need to look at present global energy production, given the decades it takes to change the energy production and distribution system [32]. Globally, fossil fuels still dominate primary energy, as they have for over a century. Although their share of electricity production is somewhat less, fossil fuels still generate nearly two-thirds of global electricity output (Table 2) (Electricity rather than primary energy data is presented here because of uncertainties regarding global bioenergy use, and conflicting methods for accounting for direct electricity production from, for example, hydro or wind [50]).

The table shows that despite rising concern about climate change, fossil fuels' share of electricity production actually increased slightly over the period 1985–2016. Both hydro and nuclear power lost share over the period, with non-hydro RE, especially wind and solar, gaining share. However, the global figures conceal vast differences between various countries. Some countries still generate all electricity from fossil fuels (e.g. Saudi Arabia and other Gulf states); some are already close to 100% from renewable energy (Iceland, Norway); in a few others nuclear power presently dominates electricity production (Belgium, France) [51].

12.3 Practical exercise no. 1

The text provided below is sourced from the literature and refers to a real OR case.[41]

> The actual production of the projects that failed in this dimension averaged a miserable 41 percent of the plan in the second six months after startup. Even worse, however, when a project suffers significant production shortfalls, a great deal of money is spent trying to rectify the problems. Although we lack the systematic data we would like, my guesstimate based on a limited data is that 25 to 50 percent added cost over the initial capital is common. Most of this is not actually capitalized, and in many cases, there are no reliable records of the amount spent at all – because nobody actually wants to know ...
>
> The effects of production problems can be debilitating for a business. One global chemical company client had a $9 billion per year business earning 22 percent return on capital employed (ROCE) – a very nice commodity business. A single megaproject that failed to produce as planned reduced the ROCE from 22 to 16 percent for the five years after the project was supposed to have started. They ended up divesting the business. Another example is a metals project that was to debottleneck and expand a major processing complex by 90 percent. After a 39 percent overrun (76 percent nominal) and an 85 percent schedule slip, the complex actually produces 10 percent less than before the project. This project managed to achieve the unachievable: negative production!
>
> When megaprojects fail, the results are rarely publicized unless the failure is spectacular. When the failures do make the press, they are damaging to a company's reputation. Large overruns and delays in cash flow due to schedule slippage or production shortfalls jeopardize the sponsor's ability to fund other projects in its portfolio. Megaprojects are by nature lumpy investments. Only a handful of companies in the world are large enough to be able to support a genuine portfolio of these projects to spread the risk internally, which is why most industrial megaprojects are joint ventures.

- From a project delivery perspective, discuss the main business and/or operational challenges that transpire here. How will such challenges affect business viability?

- What recommendations will you make to the heads of Planning and Operations?
- Discuss how such challenges might manifest (have been manifesting) themselves in the context of your organisation or in any particular project and/or programme;
- Discuss what should be done in your organisation and/or project to prevent such challenges from arising. Would you support the adoption of an OR Framework?

Wouldn't you also revert to prayer every time operability failure strikes? – If not, then you should fix your Operational Readiness processes ...

12.4 Practical exercise no. 2

This case is based on a real "operability failure" situation as discussed by Kossiakoff.[32]

Facilities and personnel limitations

Neither the facilities nor the personnel assigned to the task of system installation and test are normally equipped to deal with significant difficulties. Funds are inevitably budgeted on the assumption of success. And, while the installation staff may be experienced with the installation and test of similar equipment, they are seldom knowledgeable about the particular system being installed until they have gained experience during the installation of several production units. Moreover, the development contractor staff consists of field test engineers, while systems engineers are seldom assigned until trouble is encountered, and when it is, the time required to select and assign this additional support can be costly. The lesson to be learned is that the installation and test part of the life cycle should be given adequate priority to avoid major program impact. This means that particular attention to systems engineering leadership in the planning and execution of this process is a necessity. This should include the preparation and review of technical manuals describing procedures to be followed during installation and operation.

Early system operational difficulties

Like many newly developed pieces of equipment, new systems are composed of a combination of new and modified components and are therefore subject to an excessive rate of component failure or other operational problems during the initial period of operation, a problem that is sometimes referred to as "infant mortality".

This is simply the result of the difficulty of finding all system faults prior to total system operation. Problems of this type are especially common at external system interfaces and in operator control functions that can be fully tested only when the system is completely assembled in an operational setting. During this system shakedown period, it is highly desirable that a special team, led by the user and supported by developer engineers, be assigned to rapidly identify and resolve problems as soon as they appear. Systems engineering leadership is necessary to expedite such efforts, as well as to decide what fixes should be incorporated into the system design and production, when this can best be done, and what to do about other units that may have been already shipped or installed. The need for rapid problem resolution is essential in order to effect necessary changes in time to resolve uncertainties regarding the integrity of the production design. Continuing unresolved problems can lead to stoppages in production and installation, resulting in costly and destructive impact on the program.

In-service support

Operational Readiness testing

Systems that do not operate continuously but that must be ready at all times to perform when called upon are usually subjected to periodic checks during their standby periods to ensure that they will operate at their full capability when required. An aircraft that has been idle for days or weeks is put through a series of test procedures before being released to fly. Most complex systems are subjected to such periodic readiness tests to ensure their availability. Usually, readiness tests are designed to exercise but not to fully stress all functions that are vital to the basic operation of the system or to operational safety.

- On the above insert, underline and discuss any sections that could pertain to one of your projects. What recommendations could have been made to "Operations"?
- Discuss whether the true story below relates to Operational Readiness or rather to Operational Excellence – or perhaps to both;

When John Egan joined Jaguar in April 1980 as chairman and chief executive losses had been running at about $3 million a month. The situation was grave. His brief from the British Leyland parent board was blunt – either stop the losses and get on a profit course or close the business. Under Egan's direction Jaguar set about developing a quality control programme intended to turn the business around. Now nearly four years later, the dramatic effect of that programme can be seen in Jaguar sales, the raising of morale, and the boost of wages. [37]

12.5 Practical exercise no. 3

This scenario involves "teaching and learning" operations at a fictitious high school.

ZuQS Platinum, a global mining company operating in Southern Africa, had decided to establish the Thuto Pele Education Trust (T-PET) which will serve as a conduit to promote free high-quality education in the region. Their first initiative included a "boy-only" boarding school, the Ditaung High School, situated at some 27 km north of Mahikeng (North-West Province, South Africa). The school consisted of five 20-learner classes, libraries and laboratories, an assembly-dining hall, as well as a dormitorium (Thabo's Home) to accommodate learners from South Africa, Namibia, Botswana, Zimbabwe, and other Southern African Development Community (SADC) countries.

After two years of smooth operations, following a steady lobbying by gender-equality groups, the Trust decided to add 10 more classes, upgrade Thabo's Home from a 100- to a 150-bed capacity, and construct a brand new 150-bed dormitorium (Winnie's Home) for girls who will henceforth attend the school. Furthermore, the school has expanded its assembly-dining hall (The Lekgotla Hall) to accommodate 400+ people; the catering job (400 meals, 3 times/ day) is outsourced to Moji-le-Dijong, who are also supplying catering to the majority of ZuQS Platinum mines in the surrounding areas.

The next phase of this expansion, which is already under construction, will consist of upgrading and expanding the libraries and laboratories, the sports field, the gymnasium – to be completed by October this year.

Question no. 3.1

From an Operational Readiness perspective, assuming the said physical infrastructure is all suitably designed and constructed, what organisational *adjustments* should have been considered?

- Discuss the school as a "system" (i.e., interacting elements that serve a common purpose) and answer the above question based on Beer's Viable System Model;
- Answer the same question based on Porter's Value Chain Model provided below (Figure 12.1);
- Discuss which of these models is more suitable and provides the best outcome.

Question no. 3.2

Assuming the SA Department of Basic Education (DBE) insists that *Ditaung High School* would not be issued a "Licence to Operate" under the new operational set-up (i.e., 300+ boys and girls) unless and until a satisfactory submission is made to DBE (including Emergency Plans) that complies with the Crisis, Disaster & Emergency Act of 2017.

The Act stipulates that any new facility where more than 120 people assemble that is located more than 20 km of the nearest municipal police or fire station, shall provide its own fire and/or emergency processes and facilities. How will your team advise the school about compliance?

- Should you have known about such a requirement before the school elected to expand its operations and include a girl section, what would you have advised the school board as a possible way forward?
- Discuss, from an Operational Readiness point of view, any reasons why the school could/should disagree with the Department of Basic Education;

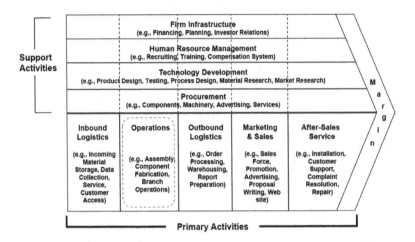

Figure 12.1 A version of Porter's Value Chain Model

- Draft an elementary Emergency Plan for the facility, discussing its key elements and implications thereof to the normal functioning of the school routines (e.g., teaching and learning)?

12.6 Practical exercise no. 4

This scenario reflects Operational Readiness issues in a hospital expansion project.

PhilaFuthi Hospital is operating at full capacity in the remote Eastern Cape, 240 km from East London; the 70-bed medical facility has served the local communities for years providing free and specialised paediatric care. The provincial government of the Eastern Cape has now allocated some R1.7 billion for the urgent rehabilitation and expansion of the hospital – which should become self-funded within a 7-year period. The approved plan consists of (1) upgrading and expanding the existing paediatric hall from the current derelict 70-bed to a fully-equipped 200-bed facility, (2) building a modern 40-bed maternity ward, and (3) building an "out-patient" facility specialising in communicable diseases such as tuberculosis and HIV/AIDS.

At this stage, it is assumed that PhilaFuthi Hospital will reach full capacity within 6 months, reaching its self-funded target way before the required 7-year period. These projections are based on the current "turn-away rate" (i.e., number of patients sent back home and/or referred elsewhere due to a lack of capacity) and the increasing incidence of communicable diseases in the region, especially among the youth.

However, the proposed funding is largely based on some cursory "feasibility study" conducted by hospital administration itself and the allocated budget will only cover the infrastructure part of the project, which is scheduled to take 28 months (including feasibility study, design, construction, and close-out).

Question no. 4.1

Considering the Operational Readiness Requirements as summarised in Table 12.1 (see page 91), answer the following questions:

- Does PhilaFuthi Hospital stand a chance of turning "self-funded" within the said 7-year period? Given the above summary, what infrastructure-related items seem to have been ignored/left out? What will be the impacts of such oversight?
- What considerations shall have changed, had this facility been located close to another (currently running) general hospital? Or, alternatively, close to a shopping mall?
- Would you have the same discussions with the hospital management team, whether the project be at FEL-1 (Conceptual Phase) or FEL-3 (Feasibility Phase)?

Question no. 4.2

In order to approach the Department of Environmental Affairs for Waste Disposal permits, please use the template provided below to summarise the Waste Disposal Strategy/Plan for PhilaFuthi Hospital.

No.	Waste item	Hazardous/polluting effects	Disposal frequency	Disposal method
01				
02				
03				
04				
05				
06				

- What adverse consequences would you anticipate should the hospital proceed with the planned expansion without attempting to reduce

Table 12.1 Operational Readiness domains and considerations

Primary OR Domain	OR Domain's aspects	OR Domain considerations, as per Operating Model
Human Resources	Training & Skills Transfer	New skills required? For whom? Skill Provision Scheme?
	Human Resources Capacity	New recruits required? By when?
	Organisational Change Management	Any changes to Structure (and office space) or Culture?
Operational Support	Bulk Supply/Services & Utilities	*New, extra Water/Electricity Supply, Sewerage needed?*
	Logistics, Supply Chain Management	*Wherewithal to procure/dispatch goods, services needed?*
	Customer/Commercial Agreements	*Are off-take contracts in place for end-products/services?*
	Financials (Δ Working Capital, Budget)	*Additional funds needed to support "added" operations?*
	Configuration Management	*How to maintain current & accurate versions of data?*
	SOMAR – *ilities*	*Any set-up to allow system to operate in its environment?*
System/Product Utilisation	Operational Health & Safety & Security	*What HSS and Continuity regimens are needed for safe utilisation?*
	Operational Licensing & Permitting	*Any Operating Licence, Waste Disposal Permit needed?*
	Technology Integration & ICT platforms	*How to align ERP, other systems to new load/technology?*
	System/Product Testing	*What testing process, equipment & components needed?*
Facilities & Tools *(considering property & facilities management)*	Operations Facilities	*Facilities, equipment, F&F, tie-ins needed for operations?*
	Spare Parts and/or Components	*Any spares, feedstock needed for testing, for operations?*
	Maintenance Facilities and Equipment	*Any facilities, plants, equipment needed for maintenance?*
Processes & Procedures	Maintenance Regime & Plans	*What types, scope, budget, and timing of maintenance?*
	Operational Risk Management	*What operational risk to mitigate? Manuals needed?*
	Warrantees Management	*What types, scope & processes? Whose responsibility?*

its "Waste Footprint"? Which stakeholders are likely to benefit/suffer the most in that woeful scenario?

- What practical measures (e.g., policy, infrastructure, processes, personnel) should be taken by the hospital in a bid to reduce the "Waste Footprint" of this facility?

Question no. 4.3

PhilaFuthi currently recycles 8 m³ of solid waste per day using their own R17.4 m (12 m³/day capacity) Waste Treatment Plant (WTP); the planned expansion might generate some additional 5 m³ of solid waste per day. Considering WTPs come in "standard" 12 m³/day capacity modules, complete the table below and discuss the effectiveness of investing in additional WTPs – and smarter investment(s) options.

Status	Volume	Plant capacity	Cost factor	Plant utilisation	Cost effectiveness	Comments
Before						
After						

Question no. 4.4

Given the planned architecture and operations of PhilaFuthi, use the provided template to work out an "Annual" Maintenance Plan, reflecting both routine and capital maintenance regimes applicable to hospital operations and the environment.

No.	Facility/ equipment item	Rationale/ purpose	Maintenance scope	Frequency	Budget
01					
02					
03					
04					
05					
06					
		Routine Maintenance Costs [A]			
01					
02					
03					
04					
05					
		Capital Maintenance Costs [B]			
	Total "Annual" Maintenance Costs [C = A + B]				

- How would you compare the costs of routine against capital maintenance, and "annual" maintenance against total capital outlay? What would you recommend?
- Can a lack of routine maintenance render void capital maintenance, or vice versa?

Personal reflections

References

1. Akam, M., 1998. Hox genes, homeosis and the evolution of segment identity: no need for hopeless monsters. *International Journal Developmental Biology*, 42(3), pp.445–451.
2. Al-Ahmad, W., Al-Fagih, K., Khanfar, K., Alsamara, K., Abuleil, S. and Abu-Salem, H., 2009. A taxonomy of an IT project failure: root causes. *International Management Review*, 5(1), pp.93–99.
3. BA Experts, 2012. *What are business, stakeholder, and solution requirements?* [online video] Available at: https://www.youtube.com/watch?v=QmCU68Vnrdg [Accessed 28 April 2018].
4. Bahill, A. and Madni, A., 2017. *Tradeoff decisions in system design.* Switzerland: Springer International Publishing, p.476.
5. Bar-Yam, Y., 2014. When systems engineering fails – toward complex systems engineering. *International Journal of System Engineering.* Cybernet. 2. 2021 - 2028 vol.2. 10.1109/ICSMC.2003.1244709
6. Bellingham, R., 2001. *The manager's pocket guide to corporate culture change.* Amherst, MA: HRD Press.
7. Bogdănoiu, C., n.d. *Business process reengineering method versus Kaizen method.* [ebook] Bucharest, Romania: Spiru Haret University. [online] Available at: http://www.cesmaa.eu/awards/BestStudentPaper_BogdanoiuCristiana.pdf [Accessed 12 June 2018].
8. Bourne, L., 2007. *Avoiding the successful failure.* Mosaicprojects.com.au. [online] Available at: https://mosaicprojects.com.au/Resources_Papers_046.html [Accessed 29 April 2018].
9. Bourne, L., 2010. Why is stakeholder management so difficult? In: *EAN University Virtual Conference.* Bogota, Columbia, p.123. [online] Available at: https://mosaicprojects.com.au/Resources_Papers_123.html [Accessed 29 April 2018].
10. Boyd, A., 2014. *Oxcal terminal 2 operational readiness low res v5 0.* [online video] Available at: https://www.youtube.com/watch?v=FlkGL4989iw [Accessed 29 April 2018].
11. Covert, M., 1997. *Successfully performing BPR.* Perth: Visible Systems Corporation.

12. Deloite & Touche, 2012. *Effective operational readiness of large mining capital projects.*

13. Dictionary of Military and Associated Terms, 2001. [ebook] Department of Defence, p.345. [online] Available at: http://www.dtic.mil/doctrine/jel/doddict [Accessed 29 Apr. 2018].

14. Dodder, S.R., Sussman, S.M. and McConnell, J.B., 2005. The concept of the CLIOS process: integrating the study of physical and policy systems sing Mexico City as an example.

15. Earley, J., 2016. *The lean book of lean – a concise guide to lean management for life and business.* 1st ed. West Sussex, Wiley.

16. Espejo, R. and Gill, A., 2015. *The viable system model as a framework for understanding organizations.* Phrontis Limited & SYNCHO Limited. [online] Available at: https://www.researchgate.net/publication/265740055_The_Viable_System_Model_as_a_Framework_for_Understanding_Organizations [Accessed 29 April 2018].

17. Espejo, R. and Harnden, R., 1989. *The viable system model - interpretations and applications of Stafford Beer's VSM.* Chichester, England: John Wiley & Sons.

18. Ferguson, A., 2014. *MSP for dummies.* Chichester, England: John Wiley & Sons.

19. Forsberg, K., Mooz, H. and Cotterman, H., 2005. *Visualizing project management.* 3rd ed. New York: John Wiley & Sons.

20. Fossnes, T. and Forsberg, K., 2006. *Systems engineering handbook a guide for system life cycle processes and activities.* 3rd ed. [ebook] Seattle, WA: INCOSE. [online] Available at: http://disi.unal.edu.co/dacursci/sistemasycomputacion/docs/SystemsEng/SEHandbookv3_2006.pdf [Accessed 29 April 2018].

21. Gould, S.J., 1996. *The mismeasure of man.* Ed. New York: Norton.

22. GP Strategies, 2016. *Operational readiness and operational excellence.* [online video] Available at: https://www.youtube.com/channel/UCMdcU5JY7QuxsX5UP-I5KzQ [Accessed 29 April 2018].

23. Haskins, C. and Forsberg, K., 2011. *Systems engineering handbook.* Seattle, WA: INCOSE.

24. Helfrich, N., 2018. *Operational readiness: 3 keys to a successful takeoff or any large-scale system.* Blog.celerity.com. [online] Available at: http://blog.celerity.com/operational-readiness-3-keys-to-a-successful-takeoff [Accessed 29 April 2018].

25. INCOSE, 2012. *Guide for the application of systems engineering in large infrastructure projects.* 1st ed. San Diego, CA: INCOSE. [online] Available at: https://www.incose.org/docs/default-source/Working-Groups/infrastructure-wg-documents/guide_for_the_application_of_se_in_large-infrastructure-projects-2012-0625-to-approved-update-2013-0417.pdf?sfvrsn=bc2c82c6_10 [Accessed 29 April 2018].

26. ISO/IEC 15288:2008, 2008. *Systems and software engineering — System life cycle processes.* 2nd ed. Geneva.

27. ISO 21500:2012, 2012. *Guidance on project management.* 1st ed. South Africa.

28. Jones, H., 2011. *Taking responsibility for complexity - how implementation can achieve results in the face of complex problems.* 2nd ed. [ebook] London: Overseas

Development Institute. [online] Available at: https://www.odi.org/sites/odi.org.uk/files/odi-assets/publications-opinion-files/6485.pdf [Accessed 29 April 2018].

29. Kalamo, R., 2012. *The balanced scorecard as a connection between strategic and operational management.* [ebook] London. [online] Available at: http://evst-mobility.eu/projectuploads/42/Balanced%20Scorecard%20as%20connection%20between%20strategic%20and%20operational%20management [Accessed 16 June 2018].

30. Kasser, J., 2015. *Creating innovative solutions to complex problem.* 2nd ed. Bedfordshire: Createspace Independent Pub.

31. Kawalek, P. and Wastell, D., 1999. A case study evaluation of the use of the viable system model in information systems development. *Journal of Database Management,* 10(4), pp.24–32.

32. Kossiakoff, A., Sweet, W., Seymour, S. and Biemer, S., 2011. *Systems engineering.* 2nd ed. Hoboken, NJ: Wiley-Interscience.

33. Mabelo, P.B., 2016. *Application of systems engineering concepts as enhancements to the project lifecycle methodology.* Masters. University of Witwatersrand.

34. Mabelo, P.B. and Sunjka, B., 2017. Application of systems engineering concepts to enhance project lifecycle methodologies. *South African Journal of Industrial Engineering,* 28(3), pp.30–45.

35. Maqsood, T., Finegan, A. and Walker, D.H.T., 2009. A conceptual model for exploring knowledge channelisation from sources of innovation in construction organizations: extending the role of knowledge management. *Proceedings of the 19th Annual ARCOM Conference, University of Brighton, 3–5 September 2003.* Reading: ARCOM, ISBN 0953416186

36. Martin, J., 2004. 3.1.2 the seven samurai of systems engineering: dealing with the complexity of 7 interrelated systems. *INCOSE International Symposium,* 14(1), pp.459–470.

37. Mayon-White, B., 1990. *Study skills for managers.* London: SAGE Publications Ltd, p.53.

38. Meadows, D. and Wright, D., 2009. *Thinking in systems.* London: Chelsea Green Publishing.

39. Meadows, D., Randers, J. and Meadows, D., 1972. *The limits to growth.* White River Junction, VT: Potomac Associates, pp.91–92.

40. Meredith, J. and Mantel, S., 2009. *Project management.* New York: Wiley.

41. Merrow, E., 2011. *Industrial megaprojects.* 1st ed. Wiley.

42. Moriarty, P. and Honnery, D., 2018. Energy policy and economics under climate change. *AIMS Energy,* 6(2), pp.272–290. doi: 10.3934/energy.2018.2.272. [online] Available at: http://www.aimspress.com/journal/energy (downloaded 02 May 2018).

43. Msengana, L., 2012. *The missing link in projects.* Randburg: Know Res Publishing.

44. NETLIPSE, 2008. *Managing large infrastructure projects (research on best practices and lessons learnt in large infrastructure projects in Europe).* NETLIPSE Report. [online] Available at: http://netlipse.eu/netlipse [Accessed 15 September 2014].

45. Oehmen, J., (ed.). 2012. *The guide to lean enablers for managing engineering programs, version 1.0*. Cambridge, MA: Joint MIT-PMI-INCOSE Community of Practice on Lean in Program Management. [online] Available at: http://hdl.handle.net/1721.1/70495 [Accessed 24/10/2019].

46. Office of Government Commerce, 2010. *Portfolio, programme and project management maturity model (P3M3®), version 2.1*.

47. Peterson, M., 2009. Bhopal plant disaster – situation summary. *International Dimensions of Ethics Education in Science and Engineering*, 1.

48. Porter, M., 2012. *Strategy and the new competitive advantage: creating shared value.* [ebook] Boston, MA: Harvard Business School, p.11. [online] Available at: https://www.hbs.edu/faculty/Publication%20Files/20121009%20-%20UDEM%20CSV%20Presentation%20-%20FINAL%20for%20Distribution_6be7f280-6a23-4b86-bcee-9af706c7ed5c.pdf [Accessed 29 April 2018].

49. Project Managers Institute, 2013. *A guide to the project management body of knowledge (PMBoK guide)*, 5th ed. Pennsylvania: Project Management Institute.

50. Scott, Z., 2012. *9 laws of effective systems engineering*. White Paper. Virginia: Vitech Corporation. [online] Available at: http://www.vitechcorp.com./resources/white_papers. [Accessed 25 June 2016].

51. Shukla, R., 2014. Review of major companies merger failures in the first decade of 21st century. *International Journal of Enhanced Research in Management and Computer Applications*, 3(3), pp.1–5.

52. Slack, N., Brandon-Jones, A. and Johnston, R., 2010. *Operations management.* 6th ed. Harlow: Prentice Hall-Financial Times.

53. *Systems engineering handbook*, 2007. 1st ed. [ebook] Washington, DC: NASA. [online] Available at: https://www.nasa.gov/sites/default/files/atoms/files./nasa_systems_engineering_handbook.pdf [Accessed 29 April 2018].

54. Thomas, A., 2008. *Business process change relevant to acca qualification paper.* Posted by BPP Learning Media. P.3.

55. Tonchia, S. and Tramontano, A., 2004. *Process management for the extended enterprise*. Berlin: Springer.

56. Torday, J., 2015. Homeostasis as the mechanism of evolution. *Biology*, 4(3), pp.573–590.

57. Widman, J., 2008. *Lessons learned: IT's biggest project failures*. PCWorld. [online] Available at: https://www.pcworld.com/article/152103/it_project_failures.html [Accessed 29 April 2018].

58. World Bank. 2014. *Public-private partnerships: Reference Guide Version 2*. World Bank, Washington, DC. © World Bank. https://openknowledge.worldbank.org/handle/10986/29052 License: CC BY 2.0 IGO

59. Yahiaoui, A. and Sahraoui, A.-E.-K., 2015. Using systems engineering practices for distributed control and building performance simulation. *INCOSE International Symposium*, pp.1290–1304. doi: 10.1002/j.2334 -5837.2015.00130.x.

60. Yetton, P., Johnston, K. and Craig, J., 1994. *Computer-aided architects*. Sydney, NSW: Australian Graduate School of Management, University of New South Wales.

Additional readings

1. Baccarini, D., 1996. The concept of project complexity – a review. *International Journal of Project Management*, 14(4), pp.201–204.

2. Cooke-Davies, T. and Patton, L.C., 2011. *Aspects of complexity: managing projects in a complex world.* Pennsylvania: Project Management Institute.

3. Cushman, M., Venters, W., Cornford, T. and Mitev, N., 2002. Understanding sustainability as knowledge practice. *Presented to British Academy of Management Conference: Fast-Tracking Performance Through Partnerships*, 9–11 September 2002, London, UK.

4. Fryer, P., 2016. *What are complex adaptive systems? A brief description of complex adaptive systems and complexity theory.* Massachusetts: Trojan Mice. [online] Available at: http://www.trojanmice.com/articles/complexadaptivesystems.htm.

5. INCOSE Transportation Working Group, 2014. *Systems engineering in transportation projects, issue 7.0.* Issue 7.0, 6 December 2014. INCOSE. [online] Available at: http://www.incose.org/docs/default-source/TWG-Documents/incose-twg-case-study-library-7_0.pdf?sfvrsn=0.

Index